BROWNIES

BROWNIES

*Over 100 Scrumptious Recipes
for More Kinds of Brownies
Than You Ever Dreamed Of*

❖

LINDA BURUM

CHARLES SCRIBNER'S SONS ■ NEW YORK

The author and publisher wish to thank the following for permission to include their recipes: Low-Calorie Fudge Brownies, from Woman's Day Low-Calorie Dessert Cookbook by Carol Cutler, copyright © 1980 CBS Publications; Blond Brownies, from The New James Beard by James Beard, copyright © 1981 James Beard; and Whole Wheat Brownies, from Maida Heatter's Book of Great Chocolate Desserts by Maida Heatter, copyright © 1980 Maida Heatter, both reprinted by permission of Alfred A. Knopf, Inc.; Toffee Fudge Brownies, by Abby Mandel, copyright © Abby Mandel; Baked Tofu Fudge Brownies, from Juel Andersen's Tofu Kitchen by Juel Andersen, copyright © 1981 Bantam Books.

Library of Congress Cataloging in Publication Data
Burum, Linda.
    Brownies : over 100 scrumptious recipes for more kinds of brownies than you ever dreamed of.
    Includes index.
    1. Brownies (Cookery)   I. Title.
TX771.B96   1984   641.8'653   84-5378
ISBN 0-684-18138-X

1 3 5 7 9 11 13 15 17 19   F / P   20 18 16 14 12 10 8 6 4 2

Printed in the United States of America.

CONTENTS

BROWNIES

INTRODUCTION

❖

Brownies are high on the list of security foods. A generous bite of brownie, lavished with nuts or frosting, is uniquely satisfying, an experience that renews faith in life's goodness despite hard times or personal disappointment.

The original brownie, known as a bar cookie, was imported from Holland. Dutch immigrant farm wives made up brownies at the end of a work-filled day to satisfy hungry appetites. So easy to whip up a child could make them, brownies soon became favorites at bake sales, soda fountains, and lunch counters across the United States.

Emerging piping hot from an oven, brownies give off a fragrant aroma that conjures up nostalgic images: county fair bake-offs, calico-lined picnic baskets on the Fourth of July, or the freshly baked batch Mom used to have ready after school, to be eaten warm along with a glass of cold milk.

Yet much as we love brownies, their simple pleasures are easily taken for granted. On a restaurant's pastry cart, the homely brownie would look pale next to such elaborate standbys as gâteau St.-Honoré, tarte de mille-feuille, and chocolate mousse; however, the brownie is probably what's eaten in the kitchen at the Four Seasons.

Brownie cognoscenti have always known where to get a good one. For many years, New York's La Caravelle has found it imperative to have a daily supply on hand (albeit on the third tier of the pastry cart) for addicted patrons whose

cravings need satisfying. More recently, chic restaurants and elegant bakeries have been turning out their own versions. The famed Beverly Hills pastry chef Michel Richard adds Grand Marnier to his brownies.

Brownie choices are diverse and astonishing. They may be filled with cream cheese, peanut butter, or plump Georgia pecans; still more elaborate varieties include the Tweed, a rococco white chocolate brownie sprinkled with semisweet chocolate mini-morsels or even Godiva chopped chocolate. Some adventurous bakers replace flour with crushed Amaretti. And behold the light chocolate Irish Cream Brownie infused with Irish cream liqueur or the Grasshopper Brownie with a filling based on crème de menthe.

New variations seem to appear daily, each brownie connoisseur eager to outdo the next or to try out another inspiration. And this is not just the realm of the gourmet or gourmand. There are the earthly pleasures of whole wheat brownies with carob chips, brownies made with wheat germ or with granola and sunflower seeds, blending health and self-indulgence in a single bite. And there is even a low-calorie brownie.

The best part of brownie making is its simplicity—no struggling with unruly pastry bags or sticky candy thermometers, no need for a battery of copper bowls and specialized baking pans, no hard-to-clean electric mixers or blenders. Unlike more elaborate *gateaux*, even the fanciest brownies take only minutes to assemble. They are, however, guaranteed to disappear in seconds.

MAKING PERFECTLY MARVELOUS BROWNIES

❖

The sense of satisfaction and delight that comes from doing something really well is as true for brownie making as for any other creative effort.

Although generally unfettered by the painstaking demands of classic pastry technique, making excellent brownies is more than a matter of haphazardly throwing ingredients together before baking. The various ways of combining and handling the basic ingredients can produce astonishingly different results.

After baking thousands of brownies in my search for the best recipes, a few unwavering principles emerged. I am passing these principles along through the recipes themselves and in the following "Brownie Baking Fundamentals." If you ignore some of these suggestions, the end result will still be edible, of course, but probably it will not produce the intended result, so you might be missing out on a truly extraordinary brownie experience.

This is not to discourage you from experimenting. But knowledgeable experimentation is not the same as careless cooking. Even experienced cooks wanting to create their own remarkable brownies might find the following suggestions useful.

Brownie Baking Fundamentals

READ THE WHOLE RECIPE just before starting. Try to get a mental picture of what you are going to do. This will help you

proceed in an organized manner, which is very important to the success of brownies.

CHOOSE THE RIGHT PAN. Note the pan size on the recipe—usually 8 × 8, 9 × 9, or 8 × 13. If a recipe calls for an 8 × 8 pan, a 9 × 9 is *not* a good substitute. The 18 square inches of difference has a major effect on the texture and thickness of the brownie. In some cases, the brownie doesn't work at all. Moreover, the baking time will be entirely different.

PREPARE THE PAN. You may want to prepare the pan before you start anything else, especially if you are going to line the pan with parchment or foil, as described on page 12.

PREHEAT THE OVEN. Brownies should be baked in a preheated oven. The oven temperature is indicated in the upper left corner of the recipe. *If you use glass baking pans, reduce the temperature 25 degrees or follow recipe instructions exactly.* For many recipes, the first thing to do is turn on the oven, unless the dough requires chilling or a filling is to be made ahead and frozen. Also, you can heat the oven while the chocolate is cooling when a recipe calls for melted and cooled chocolate.

ASSEMBLE THE INGREDIENTS AND NECESSARY EQUIPMENT.

SIFT FLOUR IF THE RECIPE CALLS FOR IT. Brownies are very sensitive to the volume of flour used in a recipe. Occasionally, a recipe calls for a measurement like "1 cup minus 1 tablespoon flour" or "½ cup and 2 tablespoons." Why is it necessary to be so exact? Unlike cakes, which contain a large volume of liquid, or bread, in which the amount of flour used depends on the water content of the flour, *brownies need an exact volume of flour.* Just a little too much makes them dry; too little makes them a gummy mess. A single recipe can produce brownies of a totally different character, depending on whether the flour is sifted. Unsifted flour sometimes yields as much as 5 tablespoons more flour a cup than does sifted. (Try measuring a cup of flour before and after sifting just to see what happens.) To make recipes as simple as possible, I have tested them, wherever practical, with stirred flour, flour that has been fluffed with a fork before it is spooned into the cup and leveled off. There are, however, recipes that, for perfect results, require that the flour be sifted. So don't be lazy—sift.

Hint: While I was testing brownies, I

came across a tiny sifter 3 inches in diameter. It will sift the small amounts required for brownies right into your measuring cup.

USE THE RIGHT FLOUR. Cake flour, pastry flour, bread flour, and all-purpose flour, both white and wheat, are not interchangeable. While many basic cookbooks suggest substituting all-purpose flour for cake flour simply by removing two tablespoons of the all-purpose flour for each sifted cup, *this does not generally apply to brownies*. Most brownies require all-purpose flour for the right texture and structure. I tried several tests with flour substitutions of various kinds, and the results were always disappointing. For the best results, use the flour that is specified.

BUTTER AND SHORTENING ARE NOT THE SAME. Except for a slight difference in flavor, unsalted butter, salted butter, and margarine will work equally well in most brownie recipes and may be used interchangeably. Depending on which ingredient you use, adjust the amount of salt in the recipe with discretion. I do not recommend anything but unsalted butter for frostings, however. Also note that butter and margarine both contain more liquid than does solid shortening and cannot be successfully substituted for it. Since the proportion of liquid must be low in brownie baking, some recipes, especially those calling for liqueurs, will specify solid vegetable shortening such as Crisco. Pure vegetable shortening has an unobtrusive flavor and allows the flavors of the chocolate and liqueur to dominate.

USE LARGE EGGS. Eggs contain a good deal of water, and therefore the number used affects the texture of brownies. All the recipes here have been tested with eggs graded large. If you use medium, extra large, or jumbo eggs, the texture of the brownies will not be what is intended, as even the slightest change in liquid volume makes a difference.

BEAT EGGS ACCORDING TO RECIPE INSTRUCTIONS. Some recipes call for eggs beaten to the consistency of whipped cream or until a trail of egg remains on the surface when beaters are lifted. This usually requires the gradual addition of sugar to the eggs and a beating time of about eight minutes. If you have a free-standing mixer with a balloon whip, this chore is easily done. But good results can be accomplished with any hand electric mixer if you persist. And you should. The texture of brownies is affected by the volume of air beaten into the eggs. If you get tired and cheat, your brownies will suffer. When separated eggs are called for, it is easier to separate them when cold; allow them to come to room temperature before beating. If you are in a hurry and all you have are cold eggs, use this trick from Jack Lirio, a well-known San Francisco cooking teacher. Place the cold eggs in a bowl of tepid water. Slowly run hot water into the bowl to warm eggs gradually; this prevents cracking. Allow eggs to sit about 10–15 minutes. Many recipes call for whole eggs that are warmed to room temperature.

CHOCOLATE-MELTING TECHNIQUES. Chocolate scorches easily and is best melted in a *bain-marie*, a pan within another pan containing a small amount of simmering water, or in the top of a double boiler over simmering water. Don't let the water boil, or the steam that escapes will affect the texture of the chocolate adversely. Chocolate may be melted over direct heat if the heat is very low, the pan is of heavy material, there are equal amounts of butter and chocolate, or the chocolate is being melted with a liquid. It is recommended that chocolate be cooled to warm

room temperature before adding it to the brownie batter or mixing it with eggs. If you need to cool the chocolate in a hurry, simply place the melting pan in a bowl of cold water and stir the chocolate until it has cooled.

If you are melting large amounts of chocolate, such as 8 ounces of semisweet, the chocolate will melt more evenly if you break it into small, equal-sized pieces.

For most chocolate melting, I prefer a heavy small pan 4 inches in diameter. This size prevents chocolate waste, and I find that with a small, flexible spatula, it is easy to get every bit of the melted chocolate into the brownie batter.

BROWN SUGAR. These recipes are meant to be made with packed golden brown sugar unless light, dark, or turbinado is specified. When granulated sugar can be substituted, this will be noted.

FOLD BEATEN EGGS AND CHOCOLATE TOGETHER. Recipes calling for well-beaten eggs do so to create a specific texture. To retain volume in beaten eggs, follow these steps:

1. Be sure chocolate is cooled to a warm room temperature. Hot chocolate cooks the eggs and tends to deflate them.

2. Pour melted chocolate around the circumference of the beaten eggs and then, with an over-and-under motion, gently fold in chocolate, being careful not to deflate eggs.

3. Sprinkle flour lightly over the surface of the egg and chocolate mixture a little at a time before folding in flour.

4. If egg whites are to be incorporated into a batter, fold one-third of the whites carefully into the batter to lighten it before folding the batter into the whites.

FOOD PROCESSOR OR ELECTRIC MIXER? Some recipes suggest using a processor *or* an electric mixer, while others specifically suggest that an electric mixer be used. The reason is that electric mixers beat more air into butter mixtures and eggs than processors do. There are times when a processor works just fine, but in other cases the amount of air beaten into the ingredients will affect the brownies' structure. Please use the suggested equipment.

BAKING SODA AND BAKING POWDER ARE NOT INTERCHANGEABLE. Baking soda is an alkali and needs to be mixed with an acid and liquid to form the carbon dioxide gas that will make cakes and brownies rise. With its high acid content, chocolate often requires only baking soda. How-ever, depending on the other ingredients, soda alone is not always enough, so both soda and baking powder or even baking powder alone may be used. There is a big difference in these products, so don't substitute one for the other.

NUTS. Because the texture of a brownie is part of its ultimate success, the size of a nut piece is important. Some recipes call for pecan or walnut pieces, others for chopped or finely chopped nuts. Nuts taste their best when broken by hand rather than cut by a sharp blade, which urges nut oils out. It is easy to break nuts into chunks. However, it would never do to put large chunks of nuts into a tiny brownie cup or a rich brownie designed to be cut into small pieces. Furthermore, in a light-textured brownie like the Macadamia Nut Brownie, large chunks of nuts would sink to the bottom of the batter. In such cases, fine chopping with a blade is the only satisfactory method.

When decorating brownie tops, sometimes a spray of finely chopped or even ground nuts makes an attractive garnish.

For purposes of recipe clarification, here are the definitions of the nut terms:

broken: a nut half broken into thirds or quarters

chopped: nut halves broken into six to eight pieces

finely chopped: nuts chopped to the texture of short-grained rice or barley

BAKE BROWNIES IN THE CENTER OF THE OVEN. This allows better heat circulation, resulting in more evenly baked brownies. If you are baking two pans at once, remember not to let pans touch each other and not to place them directly under each other. Stagger the pans on one or two oven shelves to provide for even heat circulation.

TEST FOR DONENESS. It is difficult to give hard and fast rules for doneness. No matter how carefully the recipe is followed, there are often unforeseen factors that make baking times differ. Overbaking is the cardinal sin of brownie making. Overbaked brownies are dry and lackluster. Test for doneness by inserting a toothpick half an inch from the center or the distance suggested in the recipe. The toothpick should come out barely moist; if it is dry, the brownies are overdone. Brownies continue to cook for a while after being removed from the oven. Note that a few brownies may need to bake until dry (the recipes always point this out if that is the case), while others are done when the toothpick comes out dry about 2 inches from the edge of the pan. I have tried very hard to provide as many signs of doneness as possible so that if our ovens are not uniformly calibrated, you will be able to judge when a brownie is cooked to perfection.

Glass and metal pans cook brownies differently. It is standard baking procedure with cakes and pastries to reduce oven heat by 25 degrees when using glass or ceramic pans. This rule of thumb does not always work with brownies, however, because they are very dense and don't conduct heat as quickly as cakes and pastries. I have indicated the temperature that works best for glass pans on each recipe, but when the oven temperature is 325°F, it is best to bake brownies at that temperature and shorten the baking time by five to ten minutes.

COOL BROWNIES ON RACKS. As with cakes, even air circulation when cooling promotes an evenly textured brownie and prevents soggy undersides. Just rest the brownies in their cooking pan on a raised rack. Cooling time will vary from two hours in the winter to six in the summer.

STORE BROWNIES CAREFULLY. Brownies are likely to dry out if left unwrapped or

if casually left uncovered in a frost-free refrigerator, the kind that sucks the moisture out of both the refrigerator and its contents.

I like to store brownies in a tightly covered tin with a piece of apple to help them retain moisture. Or if you don't have a tin, wrap the brownies taken from the pan first in plastic wrap and then generously in foil. After that, place them in a plastic bag. If you're storing brownies in their pan, they keep best tightly covered with foil and unrefrigerated for up to three days. After that, they should be refrigerated but served at room temperature. Brownies may be frozen, but those with a high proportion of butter or chocolate become slightly gummy, although their taste is not affected. Slightly cakier brownies will freeze well if tightly wrapped.

Measuring Ingredients

Many butter or margarine wrappers have measurements indicated on them, and the easiest way to measure is to cut off the required number of tablespoons, as shown (⅛ of a quarter-pound stick = 1 tablespoon). The following information may make measuring quicker:

BUTTER OR MARGARINE

¼ pound = ½ cup or 8 tablespoons (1 stick)
½ pound = 1 cup (2 sticks)
1 pound = 2 cups (4 sticks)

SHORTENING, FLOUR, AND SUGAR

In measuring 6 tablespoons shortening, flour, or sugar, you can measure ¼ cup (4 tablespoons) and add an additional 2 tablespoons. If a recipe calls for 7 tablespoons, measure off a ½ cup and remove 1 tablespoon. Don't use the water-displacement method to measure shortening for brownies. Even one extra drop of liquid clinging to the shortening will alter the brownie's texture.

1 cup = 16 tablespoons
½ cup = 8 tablespoons
¼ cup = 4 tablespoons
⅓ cup = 5 tablespoons

EGGS

1 large egg, beaten = 4 tablespoons beaten egg
½ egg, beaten = 2 tablespoons beaten egg

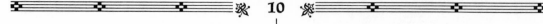
CHOCOLATE

Each brand of chocolate differs in design. Most popular brands can be measured by following these instructions:

Baker's unsweetened   Hershey's
or semisweet   unsweetened

     1 ounce   1 ounce

  ½ ounce   ½ ounce

Baker's German's Sweet

   1 ounce   2 ounces

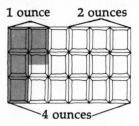

    4 ounces

Tobler semisweet and extra bittersweet

   1 ounce   2 ounces

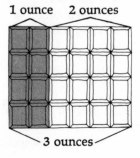

   3 ounces

1 cup semisweet chocolate morsels, regular size = 6 ounces
½ cup = 3 ounces
¼ cup plus 1 rounded tablespoon = 2 ounces
3 level tablespoons = 1 ounce

Chocolate Information for Brownie Bakers

There are so many books, not to mention a newsletter, giving helpful and loving lore on chocolate and its use in cooking that I'll restrict this discussion of chocolate to brownie baking.

Most recipes call for unsweetened chocolate, semisweet chocolate, or semisweet chocolate morsels; occasionally, one calls for Baker's German's Sweet Chocolate, cocoa, milk chocolate, or white chocolate. For best results in brownie baking, never interchange these chocolates. Although semisweet chocolates may be used in place of an equivalent amount or slightly more of chocolate morsels, both flavor and texture of the brownie will be affected. Similarly, Baker's German's Sweet, Hershey's special dark bars,

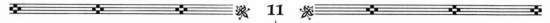
milk chocolate, and white chocolate all produce different results when substituted for semisweet chocolate.

The American passion for chocolate is now catered to by a burgeoning variety of domestic and imported chocolate. For brownies that use a high proportion of semisweet chocolate, such as the Indescribable Brownies, the Chocolate Mousse Brownies, the Big Fudge Cups, or the Grand Marnier Brownies, you might want to treat yourself to a luxury chocolate such as L'Abbaye, Tobler (semisweet or extra bittersweet), Lindt, Callebaut, Suchard, Moreau, or Guittard. I have found these brands of bittersweet and semisweet to be interchangeable; any of them will produce the same texture. Nevertheless, the flavor varies, depending on the chocolate.

Other cooks recommend Ghirardelli, Neuhaus, Nestlé's semisweet bars, or Maillard's Eagle Sweet bars. I have not personally tested with these brands. I'm sure there are others—Lanvin, for example—that are also good. Here's an area where you might want to have some fun experimenting yourself. The semisweet chocolates used for testing most of the recipes in this book were Baker's, Callebaut, Tobler, and Lindt.

In recipes calling for cocoa, Dutch processed is preferable. Droste and Poulain are two good brands.

THE PERFECT TOUCH

MAKING BROWNIES BEAUTIFUL

Here are a few pointers for making your perfect brownies perfectly beautiful. Perhaps this advice falls into the category of gilding the lily, but it's nice to have the brownies emerge from the pan with neat, clean edges.

Preparing Pans

A light pan coating of butter or shortening or a film of vegetable or lecithin spray is sufficient for most brownies. If pans are lined with parchment or foil, brownies can easily be removed in one piece and more easily cut into precise shapes. Once removed from the pan, brownies may be frosted or glazed and then neatly trimmed and attractively cut.

PARCHMENT LINING. Lay the baking pan upside-down on a work surface. Cut a strip of baking parchment to fit the exact width of the pan and a length to cover the bottom and two sides of the pan. Don't worry about the other two pan sides. Reverse the pan and lightly grease or spray it with pan coating. Fit the parchment into the pan, covering the bottom and two sides, pressing the paper firmly against the crease joining pan bottom and sides. Lightly butter the paper by brushing or wiping it with melted butter or shortening or spraying the paper with additional pan coating.

FOIL LINING. Cut a piece of foil large enough to cover the bottom and sides of

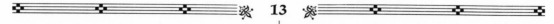
the baking pan. Turn the pan upside-down on a work surface. Press foil around the pan to conform to its shape. Turn the pan right side up, and lightly grease a 2-inch area in the center. Press foil gently into place with the side of your fingers to avoid tearing. Brush or wipe foil with melted butter or margarine, or spray with pan coating.

Removing the Brownies

Do not remove brownies until they have reached room temperature, inside as well as outside. Feel the pan bottom to determine this. Using a table knife, loosen the unlined edges of brownie and then the lined edges between the paper and pan. Wet a kitchen towel with very hot water. Place the pan on the folded towel for about half a minute. Remove the pan from the towel and, grasping the edges of the paper, wriggle it to loosen where possible. Cover the brownies loosely with plastic wrap or wax paper. Over the pan and paper place a baking sheet, cutting board, or plate large enough to accommodate the brownies lying absolutely flat (pan corners should not touch edges of plate), and invert the brownies.

Gently peel away the paper. Cover the brownies with another piece of plastic or wax paper, and invert again so that brownies are upright.

If the pan has been lined with foil, follow the above procedures, but loosen all paper-lined sides of the pan before wriggling and inverting the brownies.

When unlined pans are used, cut the brownies into quarters; loosen them from the pan edges, and with a pancake turner, remove them one-quarter at a time to a plate or piece of plastic wrap on a work surface. This way the brownies can be easily trimmed and cut into the desired shapes.

Cutting and Shaping

A brownie can be made beautiful simply by the way it is cut. Trim, neat squares are the usual shape. Sometimes brownies develop dry, uneven edges during baking that are best trimmed away. If you want to trim unfrosted brownies that have been removed from a paper-lined baking pan, it is often easiest to trim the edges while the brownie is still upside-down. First cut away the edges, then invert the brownie. Brownies can be cut into triangles by first cutting them into squares and then diagonally cutting the squares into triangles. Another appealing shape is a thin oblong about 1¾ inches long by

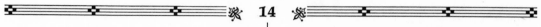
¾ inch wide. While this is nice for all types of brownies, especially when you serve a variety and want to keep each one small, this shape is especially effective for glazed and frosted brownies that are very rich.

For *even cutting* of brownie shapes, trim edges and then, using a ruler, mark guidelines by sticking toothpicks into the line at three or four intervals. Cut along these guidelines to make even strips. Then measure and mark guidelines going the opposite direction. Cut along these lines. If you're cutting brownies into small finger shapes, work with half a pan at a time. This helps prevent long strips from breaking up.

If you're cutting crusty-topped brownies or very nutty brownies, a knife with a serrated blade works best.

Frosting and Glazing

Frost first, then trim the brownie edges.

Use a large spoon to pour glaze evenly over brownie surface. Smooth with spatula when necessary. Chill the brownies thoroughly before cutting with a long, sharp, thin-bladed knife. After each cut wipe the knife blade with a damp (not wet) paper towel.

If you're glazing over a frosting, as in the Grand Marnier Brownies, be sure the frosting is well chilled before applying the glaze. Cut the brownie into long strips. Lay the strips sideways, glaze toward you, and then cut into bars. This technique works well when a filling or frosting is wedged between two baked layers as in Grasshopper Brownies or Brownie Ice Cream Sandwiches.

Improvising Decorations

NUTS. Nuts are one of the tried-and-true ways to embellish brownies. Try chopping about a quarter cup of nuts finely and sprinkling them evenly over unbaked brownie batter or over frosted brownies before cutting. Pistachios add a nice color and go well with any plain brownie. A sprinkling of slivered almonds is also good and adds visual variety when you're serving an assortment of decorated brownies. A flower design created from almond slices is another decorative use of nuts. For an attractive simple accent, press a single slice of almond into the brownie top before baking. You can stick nut slices to brownies with a glue made from a teaspoon of egg white and about 3 tablespoons of powdered sugar. If frosted, nut slices will stick to brownies by themselves.

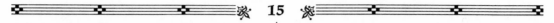
POWDERED SUGAR. A snowy frost of powdered sugar makes a finished-looking brownie when you don't want frosting. Place several tablespoons of powdered sugar into a strainer and, moving the strainer above the brownie, stir to get an even dusting of sugar. *Don't blanket brownies* with the sugar; just a dusting is best. Decorate with powdered sugar as soon before eating as possible, as the sugar may be absorbed by the moisture of the brownie.

FROSTING. A nicely swirled or rippled frosting is inviting. Use your imagination when frosting brownies.

CHOCOLATE MORSELS. Chocolate morsels, especially mini-morsels, sprinkled over frostings are a great way to gild the lily. You might try cooling a freshly baked brownie for 5 minutes and then scattering a handful of morsels over it. Be sure to allow the morsels to cool completely before you cut them. The morsels will melt slightly on their undersides and will stick to the brownies without losing their shape.

GLAZE. A quick glaze can be made by sprinkling ⅓ cup of chocolate morsels (light or dark) over an 8 × 8 or 9 × 9 pan of brownies a minute before removing the pan from the oven. After taking the pan out of the oven, allow the brownies to stand about 5 minutes before spreading the chips to a smooth glaze. Cool completely before cutting.

SPRINKLES. Chocolate sprinkles add an elegant touch—especially when contrasted against a light chocolate frosting or some such other light-colored frostings as Coffee-Brandy Buttercream and Irish Cream Frosting.

CHOCOLATE CURLS. Chocolate curls are festive looking. Shave off thin strips of chocolate with a sharp paring knife from a slightly warm semisweet bar or chunk of chocolate. Cut with a firm downward pressure against the smooth chocolate surface.

The Gift Brownie

See the suggestions for wrapping and storing brownies on page 8. For an elegant presentation, wrap brownies individually in squares of plastic wrap and then in squares of embossed florist's foil, which comes in a variety of lovely colors.

·3·

A QUEST FOR THE BEST

TWELVE RECIPES FOR
THE "PERFECT" BASIC BROWNIE

What makes the perfect brownie? Brownie connoisseurs frequently disagree. Some revel in a thick, moist, fudgy square, while others prefer more delicate cakelike varieties. There are those who think a brownie needs frosting, while purists maintain it interferes with the brownie's intrinsic character. Others argue that almonds are an improvement over the more commonly used walnuts, while classicists believe a brownie is corrupted by any kind of nut at all.

If I can judge from the thickness of my brownie recipe file, cooks have tried many formulas in their search for the elusive balance of ingredients to create the quintessential brownie. This quest is not unique. Epicures of all kinds have their own complex set of criteria for judging perfection. A good wine vintage is characterized by the subtle blending of fruitiness, acidity, dryness, and other flavoring overtones. Coffee lovers agree that there are no substitutes for the proper bean, the correct degree of roasting, the exact texture of the grind, the precise method of brewing, and even the kind of water used. But in each case the balance of qualities varies with the preferences of the drinker. Brownie lovers are no different.

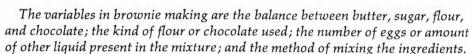

The variables in brownie making are the balance between butter, sugar, flour, and chocolate; the kind of flour or chocolate used; the number of eggs or amount of other liquid present in the mixture; and the method of mixing the ingredients.

A high ratio of butter to flour yields a dense fudgy brownie. With less butter and more flour, you'll achieve a more cakelike brownie. The proportion of sugar in the mixture affects the texture, too. More makes a gooier brownie; less, a drier one. When there is more than the average amount of chocolate in the mixture, the result is a denser brownie. Again, brownies are fudgier when the butter is melted before the other ingredients are added, unless the proportion of flour is high. When the butter is creamed before the incorporation of other ingredients, the brownie is generally more cakelike unless the amount of flour is low.

Finding the "perfect" formula is not easy and requires experimentation. One of the biggest hurdles to cross is the chocolate. How much, how bitter, and even what kind are seriously debated. A few extremists have been known to melt Godiva or Moreau chocolates to achieve the exact chocolate sensation they desire.

Clearly, different palates have varying sensibilities and requirements. With that in mind, this chapter offers twelve different basic brownie recipes, each with a slightly varied combination of those qualities that make the plain brownie so irresistible. And each one is perfect in its own right. I have stated in most of the recipes that nuts are optional, but for those who feel they are imperative, suggestions are given for quantity.

Which one is best? If you aren't quite sure what your specific requirements are, the fun lies in finding out. In your quest for the best, you may just want to try all twelve.

STANDARD ALL-AMERICAN FUDGE BROWNIE

This is the recipe I'm given most often when I'm offered someone's favorite brownie recipe. It is also the recipe I see most frequently in cookbooks, magazines, and newspapers. Although not my absolutely favorite brownie recipe, many people must consider it the best.

PREHEAT OVEN TO 350°F (325°F FOR GLASS)
8 × 8 OR 9 × 9 METAL PAN

>   2   *ounces unsweetened chocolate*
> ½   *cup butter or margarine*
>   2   *large eggs*
>   1   *cup granulated sugar*
> ¼   *teaspoon salt*
>   1   *teaspoon vanilla extract*
> ½   *cup stirred all-purpose flour*
> ⅔ to 1   *cup chopped nuts (optional)*

1. In a heavy small pan over very low heat or a double boiler, melt chocolate and butter or margarine. Stir occasionally until well blended. Remove from heat, and let cool to room temperature.

2. Beat eggs, sugar, salt, and vanilla extract together. Beat in chocolate mixture, and mix in flour. Fold in nuts, if you are using them.

3. Spray or lightly butter pan, and spread in batter.

4. If you use an 8 × 8 pan, bake in the center of the oven 20–25 minutes or until the top is dry and a wooden toothpick inserted 1½ inches from the center comes out barely moist. If you use a 9 × 9 pan, bake 18–22 minutes.

5. Cool to room temperature in the pan on a rack before cutting into desired size.

❖

EXTRA-GOOEY FUDGY BROWNIES

The almost candylike interior of these brownies inspires passionate devotees. On the other hand, they are not to everyone's liking. At a brownie tasting I staged in my living room, someone referred to them as "gummy."

PREHEAT OVEN TO 425°F (400°F FOR GLASS)
8 × 8 METAL PAN

>   4   *ounces unsweetened chocolate*
> ½   *cup unsalted butter*
>   3   *large eggs at room temperature*
>   2   *teaspoons vanilla extract*
> ¼   *teaspoon salt*
> 1⅔   *cups granulated sugar*
> ¾   *cup stirred all-purpose flour*
> 1¼   *cups walnut or pecan pieces*
>   *(optional)*

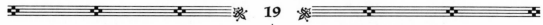
1. In a heavy medium saucepan over very low heat or a double boiler, melt chocolate and butter together. Remove from heat, and stir together until smooth and thoroughly blended. Let cool to room temperature.

2. Lightly grease or spray pan, or line with paper (see page 12).

3. In the medium bowl of an electric mixer, beat eggs, vanilla extract, and salt together until thick and light in color. Gradually add sugar, and continue to beat about 8 minutes or until eggs reach the consistency of soft peaked whipped cream and a trail of egg will remain on the surface 15 seconds when the beaters are raised.

4. Pour cooled chocolate mixture around the circumference of the eggs, and gently fold in. Fold in flour. Fold in nuts if you are using them.

5. Pour batter into prepared pan, and gently smooth top. Bake in the center of the oven 35 minutes or until the top is crisp and dry.

6. Cool completely in the pan on a rack 6 hours or overnight before cutting into 25 or 30 brownies with a long, thin, sharp knife, wiping blade after each cut.

MY FAVORITE FUDGY BROWNIE

PREHEAT OVEN TO 375°F (350°F FOR GLASS)
8 × 8 METAL PAN

> 4 ounces unsweetened chocolate
> ½ cup (1 stick) plus 1 tablespoon unsalted butter cut into 6 pieces
> 3 large eggs at room temperature
> ¼ teaspoon salt
> 1½ teaspoons vanilla extract
> ⅛ teaspoon almond extract
> 1½ cups granulated sugar
> ¾ cup sifted all-purpose flour
> 1⅓ cups walnut pieces
> powdered sugar (optional)

1. In a small pan within a larger pan over simmering water or in a double boiler, melt the chocolate. Then add the butter 1 piece at a time, stirring until each is incorporated into the chocolate. Remove from heat, mix well, and let cool to room temperature.

2. In the medium bowl of an electric mixer, beat eggs, salt, vanilla extract, and almond extract until thick and light in color. Add sugar while continuing to beat about 8 more minutes or until eggs reach the consistency of soft peaked whipped cream.

3. Thoroughly blend in chocolate mix-

ture, and then fold in flour and nut pieces.

4. Spray or lightly butter pan, and pour in batter. Bake in the center of the oven for about 35 minutes or until a wooden toothpick inserted 1½ inches from the edge comes out clean and the top is dry.

5. Cool in the pan on a rack at least 6 hours before cutting into 30 bars or 36 squares.

6. If desired, sprinkle brownies lightly with powdered sugar before serving.

BUTTERY FUDGE BROWNIES

PREHEAT OVEN TO 375°F (350°F FOR GLASS)
9 × 9 METAL PAN

> 4 *ounces unsweetened chocolate*
> ¾ *cup butter at room temperature*
> ⅛ *teaspoon salt*
> 1¼ *teaspoons vanilla extract*
> 1⅓ *cups packed golden brown sugar*
> 3 *large eggs*
> ¾ *cup stirred all-purpose flour*
> *generous cup walnut or pecan pieces (optional)*
> *powdered sugar (optional)*

1. In a small pan within a larger pan over simmering water or a double boiler, melt the chocolate. Remove from hot water, and let cool to room temperature.

2. In the medium bowl of an electric mixer, cream butter until fluffy. Add salt, vanilla extract, and brown sugar. Beat until light and creamy.

3. Add eggs one at a time, beating each in well. Beat in cooled melted chocolate on low speed. Fold in flour until just mixed. Fold in nut pieces if you are using them.

4. Spray or lightly butter pan, and pour in batter. Bake in the center of the oven 25–30 minutes or until a wooden toothpick inserted ½ inch from the center comes out barely moist.

5. Cool to room temperature in the pan on a rack. Chill before cutting into 30 bars or 36 squares.

6. If desired, sprinkle brownies lightly with powdered sugar before serving.

INDESCRIBABLE BROWNIES

Well, I'm at a loss for words when it comes to describing these indescribable

brownies, so I guess you'll just have to try these luscious chocolate squares if you want a description.

PREHEAT OVEN TO 375°F (350°F FOR GLASS)
8 × 8 METAL PAN

> 8 ounces good-quality semisweet chocolate broken up
> ½ cup unsalted butter
> 2 large eggs at room temperature
> ¼ teaspoon salt
> ⅔ cup granulated sugar
> 1 teaspoon vanilla extract
> ¼ cup stirred all-purpose flour
> 1–1¼ cups chopped walnuts or pecans powdered sugar (optional)

1. In a heavy medium saucepan over very low heat or in a double boiler, melt chocolate and butter together. Remove from heat and stir together until smooth and satiny. Let cool to room temperature.

2. In the medium bowl of an electric mixer, beat eggs until thick and light in color. Add salt, and gradually add sugar while beating about 8 minutes or until the eggs reach the consistency of soft peaked whipped cream and a trail of egg will remain on the surface 15 seconds when the beaters are raised. Beat in vanilla extract.

3. Pour cooled chocolate mixture around the circumference of the eggs, and gently fold in with an over and under motion, keeping mixture as airy as possible. Fold in flour. Fold in nuts if you are using them.

4. Spray or lightly butter pan and pour in batter. Bake in the center of the oven about 30 minutes or until a wooden toothpick inserted about 1 inch from the center comes out barely moist.

5. Cool in the pan on a rack at least 5 hours before cutting into 16 bars or 20 squares.

6. These brownies are best kept at room temperature, so do not refrigerate. To store, see instructions on page 8.

❖

TWO-WAY DEEP CHOCOLATE BROWNIES

I have found that the method used to combine brownie ingredients will affect the texture of the brownie. The first method given in this recipe produces a lighter, slightly more baked quality; the second method produces a more fudge-like texture with the same flavor. The first brownie freezes better than the second,

the second tending to become gummy if refrigerated for long periods or if frozen. Both, however, are deliciously chocolaty.

PREHEAT OVEN TO 350°F (340°F FOR GLASS)
9 × 9 METAL PAN

3	ounces unsweetened chocolate
¾	cup sifted all-purpose flour
¼	teaspoon salt
¼	teaspoon baking powder
⅔	cup butter or margarine at room temperature
1	cup granulated sugar
2	large eggs
1¼	teaspoons vanilla extract
⅔	cup nut pieces (optional)
	chocolate frosting (optional)

Method 1

1. In a small pan within a larger pan over simmering water or in a double boiler, melt chocolate. Let cool to room temperature.

2. Combine flour, salt, and baking powder; mix well.

3. In a food processor or with an electric mixer, cream butter or margarine until light. Gradually add sugar and cream until fluffy. Add eggs one at a time, beating each in well. Beat in vanilla extract and cooled chocolate. Fold in flour mixture. Fold in nuts if you are using them.

4. Spray or lightly grease pan, and pour in batter. Bake in the center of the oven 20–25 minutes or until a wooden toothpick inserted ½ inch from the center comes out barely moist.

5. Cool in the pan on a rack. When completely cool, frost if you wish. Good choices for frosting are Small-Recipe Fudge Frosting (page 154), Dark Chocolate Frosting (page 155), and Chocolate Chip Frosting (page 156). Cut into 24 or 25 brownies.

Method 2

For this method the same ingredients are used but in a different order.

1. In a heavy small pan over very low heat or in a double boiler over simmering water, melt chocolate and butter or margarine. Stir until completely mixed. Remove from heat, and let cool to room temperature.

2. Combine flour, salt, and baking powder; mix well.

3. In a food processor or with an electric mixer, beat eggs and sugar together until light. Mix in vanilla extract, melted chocolate mixture, and flour mixture. Fold in nuts if you are using them.

4. Spray or lightly grease pan, and pour in batter. Bake in the center of the oven 20–25 minutes or until a wooden toothpick inserted ½ inch from the center comes out barely moist.

5. Cool completely in the pan on a rack. When cool, frost if you wish (see above recipe). Cut into 24 or 25 brownies.

IN-BETWEEN BROWNIES

This brownie recipe uses oil to produce a fudgy yet slightly cakelike brownie.

PREHEAT OVEN TO 350°F (340°F FOR GLASS)
9 × 13 METAL PAN

    4 *ounces unsweetened chocolate*
1⅓ *cups stirred all-purpose flour*
    ¾ *teaspoon baking powder*
    ¼ *teaspoon salt*
    4 *large eggs at room temperature*
1⅔ *cups granulated sugar*
    2 *teaspoons vanilla extract*
    ⅔ *cup vegetable oil carefully*
       measured in a glass cup at eye
       level
    1 *cup walnut or pecan pieces*
       (optional)

chocolate frosting (optional)
powdered sugar (optional)

1. In a small pan within a larger pan over simmering water or a double boiler, melt the chocolate. Let cool slightly.

2. Combine flour, baking powder, and salt; mix well.

3. In a food processor or with an electric mixer, beat eggs until thick and light in color. Gradually add sugar, beating until well blended. Stir in vanilla extract, oil, and chocolate; blend well. Stir in flour mixture. Fold in nuts if you are using them.

4. Lightly grease or spray pan, and spread in batter. Bake in the center of the oven 25–30 minutes or until a wooden toothpick inserted halfway between the edge and center comes out clean.

5. Cool completely in the pan on a rack. If desired, frost or dust lightly with powdered sugar before cutting into 24 or 28 bars. Good choices for frosting are Chocolate Chip Frosting (page 156) and Small-Recipe Fudge Frosting (page 154).

BASIC FUDGE
CAKE BROWNIE

The corn syrup in this deep chocolate batter keeps the finished product moist while the brownie retains a slight cake-like quality—an excellent basic recipe.

PREHEAT OVEN TO 375°F (350°F FOR GLASS)
9 × 9 METAL PAN

> 4   ounces unsweetened chocolate
> ½   cup butter or margarine at room
>   temperature
> ¼   teaspoon salt
> ¾   cup granulated sugar
> ⅔   cup packed golden brown sugar
> ⅓   cup light corn syrup
> 3   large eggs
> 1   teaspoon vanilla extract
> 1   cup sifted all-purpose flour
> 1   cup nut pieces (optional)
>   powdered sugar, Chocolate
>   Glaze 1 (page 34), or frosting
>   of your choice (optional)

1. In a small pan within a larger pan over simmering water or a double boiler, melt chocolate. Let cool to room temperature.

2. In a food processor or with an electric mixer, cream butter or margarine, salt, and granulated sugar until light and fluffy. Add light brown sugar and beat until creamy. Beat in corn syrup, and then add eggs one at a time, beating each in well. Beat in vanilla extract and melted chocolate. Stir in flour by hand. Stir in nuts if you are using them.

3. Spray or lightly grease pan, and spread in batter. Bake in the center of the oven 30–35 minutes or until the top is dry and a wooden toothpick inserted ½ inch from the center comes out barely moist.

4. Cool completely in the pan on a rack before sprinkling with powdered sugar, glazing, or frosting, as desired. Cut into 20 or 24 bars.

❖

ADULT
CHOCOLATE BROWNIES

I refer to these as "adult" because they have less sugar and more chocolate than most brownies. They are a dense but not gooey brownie.

PREHEAT OVEN TO 325°F
9 × 9 METAL PAN

> 4   ounces unsweetened chocolate
> ½   cup unsalted butter at room
>   temperature

1¼ cups granulated sugar
¼ teaspoon salt
2 teaspoons vanilla extract
4 large eggs
⅔ cup stirred all-purpose flour
1¼ cups walnut pieces (optional)

1. In a small pan within a larger pan over simmering water or a double boiler, melt the chocolate. Let cool to room temperature.

2. Lightly grease or spray pan, or line with parchment (see page 12).

3. In a food processor or with an electric mixer, cream butter until fluffy. Add sugar in thirds, continuing to beat until mixture is light and creamy. Beat in salt and vanilla extract. Add eggs one at a time, beating in each well. Mix in melted chocolate. Fold in flour by hand. Fold in nuts if you are using them.

4. Pour batter into prepared pan. Bake in the center of the oven 22–25 minutes (17–20 minutes for glass pan) or until the top is dry and a wooden toothpick inserted 1½ inches from the center comes out barely moist.

5. Cool completely in the pan on a rack before cutting into 20 bars.

CLASSIC CAKELIKE BROWNIES

Superbly textured, moist, and chocolaty yet slightly cakelike. Very versatile— good with or without nuts and/or with or without frosting.

PREHEAT OVEN TO 350°F (340°F FOR GLASS)
9 × 9 METAL PAN

2 ounces unsweetened chocolate
⅔ cup sifted all-purpose flour
½ teaspoon baking powder
¼ teaspoon salt
¼ cup butter or margarine at room temperature
1 cup granulated sugar
2 large eggs separated and left to stand until room temperature
1 teaspoon vanilla extract
¼ cup milk
½ cup walnut pieces (optional)
  powdered sugar (optional)
  frosting (optional)

1. In a small saucepan within a larger pan over simmering water or a double boiler, melt chocolate. Remove from heat, and let cool to room temperature.

2. Spray or lightly grease pan, or if you want to remove whole cake from pan before cutting it, line pan according to directions on page 12.

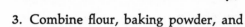
3. Combine flour, baking powder, and salt; blend well.

4. Cream the butter and sugar together with an electric mixer until light and fluffy. Beat in egg yolks one at a time; beat in vanilla extract and milk. Stir in melted chocolate and flour mixture.

5. In a separate bowl, with clean beaters, beat egg whites just until curved peaks will hold their shape. Do not overbeat. Fold one-third of the egg white mixture into the chocolate mixture, then fold in the rest of whites. Fold in nuts if you are using them.

6. Pour into prepared pan, and bake in the center of the oven 25–30 minutes or until the top is dry and a wooden toothpick inserted into the center comes out barely moist.

7. Cool completely in the pan on a rack. If you have lined the pan, invert the cooled cake onto a large plate or baking sheet, and gently peel away the paper. Turn cake over, and frost if desired. Good choices for frosting are Small-Recipe Fudge Frosting (page 154), Semisweet Chocolate Icing (page 156), Pâtissière Buttercream (page 154), and Dark Chocolate Frosting (page 155). Cut into 20 bars. You may want to dust unfrosted brownies with a little powdered sugar just before serving.

CHAMELEON BROWNIES

I call these chameleon brownies because they are the perfect frosting and filling mate. Slightly cakelike and not too sweet, they make the perfect foil for a rich fudgy frosting. Or you might want to sandwich a delicious buttercream between two layers of the brownie to create elegant brownie sandwiches. For cutting directions, see page 13. This brownie freezes well, so when you feel like a little creative expression, thaw them out and create something delicious.

PREHEAT OVEN TO 350°F (340°F FOR GLASS)
9 × 13 METAL PAN

>   3   ounces unsweetened chocolate
>   1   cup minus 1 tablespoon sifted
>   all-purpose flour
>   ¾   teaspoon baking powder
>   ¾   cup butter or margarine at room
>   temperature
>   ¼   teaspoon salt
>   1¼ cups granulated sugar
>   1½ teaspoons vanilla extract
>   3   large eggs
>   1¼ cups walnut pieces (optional)

1. In a small pan within a larger pan over simmering water or a double boiler, melt the chocolate. Let cool to room temperature.

2. Prepare pan by lining it with foil or parchment (see page 12).

3. Combine sifted flour and baking powder; mix well.

4. In a food processor or with an electric mixer, cream butter until light and fluffy. Add salt, sugar, and vanilla extract, and beat until thoroughly combined.

5. Add eggs one at a time, beating each in well. Stir in melted chocolate, and then fold in flour mixture. Fold in nuts if you are using them.

6. Spread batter into pan, and smooth the top. Bake in the center of the oven for 20–25 minutes or until the top is dry and a wooden toothpick inserted 1 inch from the center comes out barely moist.

7. Cool completely in the pan on a rack. When cool, loosen edges, and invert brownies onto a platter or baking sheet. Peel away paper, and frost bottom or fill as desired before cutting into desired size.

EXTRA-CHOCOLATE CAKELIKE BROWNIES

Rich and chocolaty but still cakelike. It is important to beat the eggs until they are like whipped cream, or the brownies will be too heavy.

PREHEAT OVEN TO 350°F (340°F FOR GLASS)
9 × 9 METAL PAN

 3 *ounces unsweetened chocolate*
 ¼ *cup butter or margarine cut into*
   4 pieces
 1 *cup sifted cake flour*
 ¼ *teaspoon baking soda*
 ¼ *teaspoon baking powder*
 ¼ *teaspoon salt*
 2 *eggs at room temperature*
 1 *teaspoon vanilla extract*
1⅓ *cups granulated sugar*
 ⅓ *cup light cream*
 ¾ *cup walnut pieces or pecan pieces*
   (optional)
   frosting (optional)

1. In a small pan within a larger pan over simmering water or a double boiler, melt the chocolate. Then add the butter one piece at a time, stirring until each piece is incorporated into the chocolate. Remove from heat; cool slightly.

2. Lightly grease or spray pan, or line as directed on page 12.

3. Combine sifted flour, baking soda, baking powder, and salt.

4. With an electric mixer, beat eggs until they are thick and light in color.

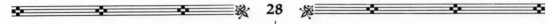

Add vanilla extract and gradually add sugar, continuing to beat about 8 minutes or until eggs are the consistency of softly whipped cream. Do not use a food processor for this recipe.

5. Pour the chocolate mixture around the circumference of the eggs, and gently fold it in.

6. Fold in one-third of the flour mixture, half of the cream, another third of the flour mixture, the remaining cream, and the remaining flour. Fold in nuts if you are using them.

7. Spread batter into prepared pan, and smooth top. Bake in the center of the oven 27–35 minutes or until the top is dry and a wooden toothpick inserted ½ inch from the center comes out barely moist.

8. Cool completely in the pan on a rack. If you have lined the pan, invert the brownies onto a plate. Peel away paper, and invert again. Frost if desired, and cut into 24 bars. Good choices for frosting are Small-Recipe Fudge Frosting (page 154), French Custard Buttercream (page 152), and Chocolate Chip Frosting (page 156).

·4·

DELUXE BROWNIES

In a manner of speaking, any well-made brownie is intrinsically deluxe. Good ingredients, care, and attention are all that's needed. Yet supposing you want to go for broke—say a special thank you to a friend, please a pampered potentate, console someone who's been laid up for a while? In this chapter we pull out all the stops, adding such luxury ingredients as French marron purée, Grand Marnier, amaretto, or Kahlúa liqueurs, and crushed Amaretti biscuits. The very names of these brownies resound with opulence and sensory gratification carried to the brink of overindulgence. Nothing but the best is used here: good sweet butter, the freshest nuts, excellent chocolate.

On a doilied plate, you might present a trio of liqueur-based brownies—the Grand Marnier, the Irish Cream, the Grasshopper (crème de menthe)—with after-dinner coffee. In a gift box to a special someone, pack miniature brownie bonbons with coffee-rum filling, Irish Coffee Brownies, or Brownies aux Marrons with their superb, trufflelike texture and crisp coating of semisweet glaze. Imagine the joy of receiving them in a heart-shaped or hand-painted container!

Given their special nature, you may wish to make your deluxe brownies as visually appealing as they are delicious by giving them a few pastry-chef touches. The techniques discussed in "The Perfect Touch" are keys to creating the most perfect-looking brownies possible.

AMARETTO BROWNIES

Reminiscent of a Viennese torte with its ground almonds, not too sweet chocolate flavor, and touch of amaretto, the almond liqueur, in the brownie and the chocolate glaze.

PREHEAT OVEN TO 350°F (340°F FOR GLASS)
9 × 13 METAL PAN

>   about 1 cup raw or roasted
>   unsalted almonds
> 9 ounces semisweet chocolate
> 6 tablespoons unsalted butter
> 6 large eggs at room temperature
> 1/8 teaspoon salt
> 1 teaspoon vanilla extract
> 2/3 cup granulated sugar
> 3 tablespoons all-purpose flour
> 2 tablespoons brandy
> 3 tablespoons amaretto
>   Amaretto-Chocolate Glaze
>   (below)
>   sliced almonds

1. If almonds are raw, roast them in the baking pan in a preheated 350°F oven for 15 minutes. Cool completely, at least an hour. Finely grind almonds in food processor or with a hand-held rotary grater (Mouli type). Use only 1 cup of ground almonds in the recipe.

2. In a heavy medium pan over very low heat or a double boiler, melt chocolate and butter together. When melted, mix thoroughly until completely smooth. Remove from heat, and cool to room temperature.

3. Beat eggs, salt, and vanilla extract until thick and light in color. Add sugar, and beat until egg mixture is pale yellow.

4. Sprinkle flour over the surface of the eggs, and fold in. Sprinkle on 1/2 cup of the nuts, and fold in. Pour melted cooled chocolate mixture around the circumference of the batter, and fold in. Fold in brandy and the remaining 1/2 cup of nuts.

5. Spray or lightly grease pan, and pour batter in. Bake in the center of the oven about 25 minutes or until the top is just dry and a wooden toothpick inserted in the center comes out barely moist. Cool to lukewarm in the pan on a rack. Loosen the edges of the cake, and invert onto a platter or board. Sprinkle slowly and evenly with 3 tablespoons of amaretto. Let sit about 2 hours, until absorbed.

6. When liqueur is absorbed, prepare the glaze (below).

7. Pour glaze evenly over the top of the cake, spreading it with a spatula. Allow the glaze to set 20 minutes before scoring the top of the cake into 24 squares

and decorating each square with a flower made from 5 or 6 almond slices. If you want to get really fancy, double the glaze recipe. Cut the brownies before glazing, remove from the pan with a spatula, place each brownie on a rack, and glaze the top and sides before decorating with the almond slices. Allow glaze to set until firm.

AMARETTO-CHOCOLATE GLAZE

    3 tablespoons water
    1 tablespoon sugar
    3 ounces semisweet chocolate
    ½ tablespoon amaretto

1. Combine water and sugar in a small saucepan, and simmer until sugar is dissolved.

2. Add chocolate, and simmer until completely melted. Stir until smooth, and simmer until glaze coats the back of a spoon.

3. Remove from heat, and stir in amaretto.

KAHLUA-CHOCOLATE CHIP BROWNIES

PREHEAT OVEN TO 350°F (325°F FOR GLASS)
8 × 8 METAL PAN

    4 ounces semisweet chocolate
    1 cup plus 2 tablespoons sifted
        all-purpose flour
    ½ teaspoon baking soda
    ½ teaspoon salt
    3½ teaspoons powdered instant
        espresso
    ⅓ cup unsalted butter at room
        temperature
    ¼ cup granulated sugar
    ½ cup packed golden brown sugar
    1 large egg
    4 tablespoons Kahlúa
    1½ teaspoons vanilla extract
    ½ cup semisweet chocolate pieces
    ½ cup chopped pecans
        Kahlúa Glaze (optional, below)

1. In a small pan within a larger pan over simmering water or in a double boiler, melt chocolate. Let cool slightly.

2. Generously grease the pan, then line the bottom and two sides with aluminum foil or parchment (see page 12). Grease paper.

3. Combine the flour, baking soda, salt, and powdered espresso. Mix well.

4. In a food processor or in the medium bowl of an electric mixer, cream the butter and sugars together until light. Add the egg, and beat well.

5. Mix in 2 tablespoons of Kahlúa, the vanilla, and the melted chocolate. Add the flour mixture, and mix just enough to blend completely.

6. Stir in the chocolate pieces and pecans. Spoon batter into the pan, spreading evenly.

7. Bake in the center of the oven about 25–30 minutes or until a wooden toothpick inserted 1 inch from the center comes out barely moist. Do not overbake.

8. Cool completely in the pan on a rack. When cool, loosen the edges of the brownie, and invert the pan onto a plate, shaking to loosen. Peel away paper.

9. Prick the bottom of the brownie at 1½-inch intervals. Sprinkle with the remaining 2 tablespoons of Kahlúa. Try to pour liqueur slowly around the edges, taking care that it does not all slide into the concave center.

10. Allow the brownie to sit, covered with foil or plastic wrap, at least 4 hours. Spread glaze over brownie if you wish. Allow brownie to sit until glaze is set. Trim dry edges from the brownie before cutting into 16 squares. These brownies are best if cut and individually wrapped.

KAHLUA GLAZE

    5–6 teaspoons *Kahlúa*
    ½ cup powdered sugar

1. Combine 4 teaspoons of Kahlúa with powdered sugar. Mix well.

2. Slowly add up to 2 more teaspoons of Kahlúa until the glaze becomes spreadable.

GRAND MARNIER BROWNIES

PREHEAT OVEN TO 325°F
9 × 9 METAL PAN

    1 *ounce unsweetened chocolate*
    6 *ounces semisweet chocolate*
    7 *tablespoons vegetable shortening*
    ⅔ *cup sifted all-purpose flour*
    ¼ *teaspoon baking soda*
    ¼ *teaspoon salt*
    2 *large eggs*
    1 *teaspoon vanilla extract*
    ⅔ *cup granulated sugar*
    2 *tablespoons Grand Marnier*
    1 *tablespoon minced or grated*
      orange zest
    ¾ *cup chopped blanched almonds*
      (optional)

Orange Buttercream (below)
Chocolate Glaze 1 (below)

1. In a heavy small pan over very low heat or in a double boiler, melt the chocolates and the shortening. Stir together until smooth; and let cool to room temperature.

2. Prepare pan by lining it with foil or parchment (page 12).

3. Combine flour, baking soda, and salt; mix well.

4. In a food processor or with an electric mixer, beat eggs until light in color. Add vanilla extract, sugar, 1 tablespoon of Grand Marnier, and orange zest. Beat until well blended.

5. Mix in chocolate mixture and then flour mixture until just blended. Fold in nuts, if you are using them.

6. Pour batter into prepared pan, and smooth top.

7. Bake for 25–30 minutes (20–25 minutes for glass pan) or until the top is shiny and a wooden toothpick inserted 1 inch from the edge of the cake comes out barely moist.

8. Cool in the pan on a rack at least 2 hours. Loosen the edges of the cake from the sides of the pan, and invert onto a plate. Peel away paper.

9. Prick the cake at 1½-inch intervals with a wooden toothpick, and evenly pour 1 tablespoon of Grand Marnier over the surface. Let stand 30 minutes; cover and chill.

10. Make Orange Buttercream, and spread smoothly over the surface of the cake. Chill again until firm.

11. Spread Chocolate Glaze over the frosting, and chill to firm. Cut into 24 bars. Remove from refrigerator about an hour before serving.

ORANGE BUTTERCREAM

    6 tablespoons unsalted butter at room temperature
2–3 teaspoons frozen orange juice concentrate thawed
    1 cup powdered sugar
1½ teaspoons minced or grated orange zest

1. Combine butter and 2 teaspoons of frozen orange juice concentrate.

2. Beat in powdered sugar and orange zest.

3. Beat in about ½ teaspoon additional orange juice concentrate to get desired consistency.

CHOCOLATE GLAZE 1

> ½ cup semisweet chocolate morsels
> or 2½ ounces semisweet
> chocolate
> 1 tablespoon butter

1. Melt chocolate and butter over hot water.
2. Stir to blend well.

❖

CREME DE MENTHE–FILLED BROWNIE BONBONS

The perfect "little" dessert—depending on how many you eat—or a delightful gift, alone or as part of an assortment of gourmet brownies. But plan ahead. The filling for these bonbons must be frozen before they can be assembled and baked.

PREHEAT OVEN TO 350°F
2 MUFFIN PANS WITH MINIATURE CUPS
(1 INCH IN DIAMETER)

> Crème de Menthe Filling (below)
> 1 ounce unsweetened chocolate
> 2 ounces semisweet chocolate
> 6 tablespoons unsalted butter
> ⅔ cup sifted cake flour
> ¼ teaspoon baking powder
> ⅛ teaspoon baking soda
> ¼ teaspoon salt
> 2 large eggs minus 2 tablespoons
> egg at room temperature*
> 1 teaspoon vanilla extract
> ⅔ cup granulated sugar
> 2 tablespoons light cream

1. Prepare Crème de Menthe Filling; freeze at least 6 hours. Reserve extra egg.
2. In a heavy small pan over very low heat or in a double boiler, melt the chocolates and butter together. Remove from heat; blend well and cool slightly.
3. Combine sifted flour, baking powder, baking soda and salt. Mix well and reserve.
4. With an electric mixer, beat reserved egg until blended. Add vanilla extract, and beat until light. Gradually beat in sugar about 1½ minutes or until mixture is thick and light colored. Beat in chocolate mixture.
5. Fold in one third of the flour mixture and half the cream. When well blended, fold in second third of the flour mixture, the remaining cream, and the remaining flour.

* If you make both filling and bonbons on the same day, beat two large eggs and use 2 tablespoons for filling and the rest for the chocolate batter.

6. Line muffin pans with paper cups, and fill about halfway, using a scant 2 teaspoons batter for each.

7. Remove one-third of the filling from the freezer. Place a rounded ½ teaspoon of filling in the center of each cup, and cover with 1 teaspoon of batter. Fill cups only three-quarters full. Remove more filling from the freezer as needed, keeping as close to frozen as possible.

8. Keep first pan of bonbons cool while you fill the second. Chill batter while waiting for the first batch of bonbons to bake.

9. Bake first batch of two pans in the center or oven about 30 minutes or until a wooden toothpick inserted three-quarters from the edge of a bonbon comes out clean.

10. Cool in their pans on racks until bonbons are firm enough to be handled. Lift from the pan by grasping the edges of the paper cups. Makes 30 bonbons.

CREME DE MENTHE FILLING

  2 ounces cream cheese softened
  4 teaspoons granulated sugar
  1 tablespoon green crème de
        menthe
  2 tablespoons egg lightly beaten
  1 tablespoon all-purpose flour

1. Beat cream cheese and sugar together until light and smooth. Blend in crème de menthe.

2. Beat eggs only until they reach a uniform yellow. Remove 2 tablespoons for the filling, and reserve the rest for the bonbon base.

3. Beat the 2 tablespoons of egg into the cheese mixture, and then beat in flour just until mixed.

4. Freeze filling until firm, at least 6 hours. The filling can be frozen up to 2 weeks, the longer the better.

COFFEE-BRANDY–FILLED BONBONS

Follow directions for Crème de Menthe–Filled Bonbons substituting this filling, made the same way as the Crème de Menthe Filling.

COFFEE-BRANDY FILLING

  2 ounces cream cheese softened
  2 tablespoons granulated sugar
  ½ teaspoon instant coffee powder
  1 tablespoon brandy
  2 tablespoons egg lightly beaten
  1 tablespoon all-purpose flour

WALNUT FANTASY

A voluptuous layer of caramelized walnuts tops a semisweet fudgy brownie.

9 × 9 METAL PAN

BROWNIE LAYER

    3   ounces unsweetened chocolate
    6   tablespoons unsalted butter
    ¼   teaspoon salt
    1   cup plus 2 tablespoons
            granulated sugar
    2   large eggs slightly beaten
    1½ teaspoons vanilla extract
    ½   cup stirred all-purpose flour

1. In a heavy medium pan over very low heat or in a double boiler, melt chocolate and butter together; cool slightly.

2. Blend in salt and sugar, then mix in eggs and vanilla extract. When mixture is completely blended, add flour.

3. Spray or lightly grease pan, and spread batter in it. Chill batter about 2 hours or until cold throughout. Do not skip this step; it is critical to the success of the recipe.

4. About 10 minutes before assembly and baking, prepare Walnut Topping.

WALNUT TOPPING

    ¼   cup unsalted butter
    ¼   cup granulated sugar
    ½   cup packed golden brown sugar
    2   tablespoons all-purpose flour
    2   eggs lightly beaten
    1½ teaspoons vanilla extract
    3¾ cups walnut pieces

1. Melt butter over low heat. When melted, stir in sugars and cook, stirring, 1 minute. Remove from heat.

2. Beat in flour and then eggs, and cook over low heat, stirring slowly about 3-4 minutes or until mixture becomes light in color.

3. Remove from heat, and stir in vanilla extract and walnut pieces. Mix to coat every nut piece.

ASSEMBLING AND BAKING

1. Preheat oven to 350°F (340°F for glass pan).

2. Drop walnut mixture in even mounds over the surface of the chocolate batter, and spread into an even layer. Do not neglect the edges. Push the walnut mixture into every corner.

3. Bake in the center of the oven 40–50 minutes or until a wooden toothpick inserted 2 inches from the center of the pan comes out free of chocolate.

4. Cool in the pan on a rack 6 hours or overnight. With a very sharp long, thin-bladed knife, carefully cut brownies into 25 squares.

TWEED BROWNIES

A white chocolate brownie with semi-sweet chocolate chips.

While testing many pans of this particular brownie, I learned that working with white chocolate is not like working with brown chocolate. For my first batch, I used a recipe calling for semisweet chocolate, and I simply substituted white chocolate. From the gooey mass that emerged from my oven, I learned that the amount of chocolate necessary for good flavor produced an entirely unacceptable texture. Finally, I solved this problem by melting only half of the chocolate and adding the balance in chopped form. I also found it impossible to make a smooth melted white chocolate and butter mixture, as is often called for in traditional recipes. But an almost uniform mixture can be achieved by adding the butter to the melted chocolate in stages, the way

you make a hollandaise sauce. Finally, I found that beating the eggs and sugar together gives a brownielike texture; if the eggs are not beaten or not beaten sufficiently, the texture will be cakelike. My brief background in food science did not prepare me to present an analysis of all this, but I *do* want to suggest that you follow the directions with care.

PREHEAT OVEN TO 350°F (340°F FOR GLASS)
9 × 9 METAL PAN

6 ounces white chocolate
(I use 2 3-ounce Lindt bars.)
½ cup unsalted butter cut into 6 pieces
2 large eggs at room temperature
¾ cup granulated sugar
½ teaspoon salt
1½ teaspoons vanilla extract
½ teaspoon almond extract
1 cup stirred all-purpose flour
½ cup semisweet chocolate mini-morsels
½ cup chopped blanched almonds

1. Generously grease the baking pan. Line the bottom and two sides with aluminum foil or baking parchment. Grease the paper and sides of the baking pan.

2. Chop 3 ounces of the chocolate

fine, until it is about the size of cooked rice or barley.

3. Melt the remaining 3 ounces of chocolate in the top of a small double boiler over moderate heat. When the chocolate is soft, add the butter one piece at a time. Stir in each piece with a fork, blending it into the chocolate completely before adding another piece. When all the butter is incorporated, remove from heat and let cool slightly.

4. In the large bowl of an electric mixer, beat eggs until very light in color. Add the sugar a little at a time, and continue beating until mixture is very thick and will leave a trail on its surface for 10 seconds when beaters are raised.

5. Beat in salt, vanilla extract, and almond extract. Add melted chocolate mixture, and fold in well. Fold in flour, chopped chocolate, ¼ cup of the chocolate mini-morsels, and almonds.

6. Spoon batter into the pan, spreading evenly. Sprinkle with remaining chocolate morsels.

7. Bake in center of the oven 30–35 minutes or until the top is dry and a wooden toothpick inserted 1 inch from the center comes out clean.

8. Cool brownies completely in the pan on a rack. When cool, loosen the edges of the brownie and the paper with a spatula. Place a large plate over the brownie and invert. Peel away paper. Trim the dry edges before cutting into 30 or 36 brownies.

IRISH CREAM BROWNIES

I used Baker's German's Sweet Chocolate and a few semisweet morsels to give a full-bodied but not overpowering chocolate flavor to complement the delicate Irish cream liqueur.

PREHEAT OVEN TO 325°F
9 × 9 METAL PAN

> One 4-ounce bar Baker's German's
>   Sweet Chocolate
> ⅓ cup semisweet chocolate morsels
> 6 tablespoons vegetable shortening
>   (not butter or margarine)
> ¾ cup sifted all-purpose flour
> ¼ teaspoon baking soda
> ¼ teaspoon salt
> 2 large eggs
> ⅓ cup granulated sugar
> 1 teaspoon vanilla extract
> 2 tablespoons brandy
> 3 tablespoons Irish cream liqueur

Irish Cream Frosting (below)
semisweet chocolate mini-morsels
(optional)

1. In a heavy small pan over very low heat or in a double boiler, melt the Baker's chocolate, the chocolate morsels and shortening. Stir until smooth, and cool to room temperature.

2. Prepare pan by lining it with foil or parchment according to directions on page 12.

3. Combine sifted flour, baking soda, and salt. Mix well.

4. In a food processor or with an electric mixer, beat eggs until light in color. Add sugar, vanilla extract, and brandy; beat until well blended.

5. Stir chocolate mixture into egg mixture, and then add flour mixture just to blend.

6. Pour batter into prepared pan and smooth top. Bake in the center of the oven 20–25 minutes (18–22 minutes for glass pans) or until the top is shiny and a wooden toothpick inserted three-quarters of the way in from the edge of the brownie comes out clean.

7. Cool in pan on a rack at least 2 hours. Loosen edges of cake from pan, and invert onto a plate. Gently peel away paper.

8. Prick the cake at 1½-inch intervals with a wooden toothpick, and evenly pour 3 tablespoons of Irish cream liqueur over the surface. Be sure each tablespoonful is absorbed before pouring on the next. Let stand 30 minutes; cover with plastic wrap and chill.

9. Make Irish Cream Frosting, and spread smoothly over the surface of the brownie. Sprinkle with chocolate mini-morsels if desired, and chill again until frosting is firm.

10. About an hour before serving, remove brownie from refrigerator, and cut into bars. (See directions for cutting frosted brownies on page 13.) Serve brownies at room temperature.

IRISH CREAM FROSTING

    2 tablespoons unsalted butter at
       room temperature
    1 egg yolk
    5 teaspoons Irish cream liqueur
    ⅔ cup powdered sugar

1. Combine butter with egg yolk and Irish cream liqueur; mix as well as possible.

2. Gradually add powdered sugar. Beat well with an electric mixer or wire

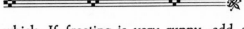

whisk. If frosting is very runny, add a little more powdered sugar. Frosting will firm up when chilled.

❖

BROWNIES AUX MARRONS

The European tradition of using chestnuts in a *gateau* is transferred here to this elegant brownie with its trufflelike texture and crisp coating of thin chocolate.

PREHEAT OVEN TO 350°F (340°F FOR GLASS)
9 X 9 METAL PAN

> 7 *ounces semisweet chocolate*
> ½ *cup unsalted butter*
> 3 *tablespoons cognac, brandy, or amber rum*
> 1 *cup (half of a 15-ounce can) chestnut purée with glucose*
> 3 *large eggs at room temperature*
> ⅔ *cup granulated sugar*
> ½ *teaspoon vanilla extract*
> 5 *tablespoons stirred cake flour Chocolate Glaze 2 (below)*

1. In a heavy medium pan over very low heat or in a double boiler, combine chocolate, butter, and cognac, brandy, or rum. Cook over very low heat until the chocolate is melted; stir to mix thoroughly. Add chestnut purée, breaking up any chunks with a fork. Blend until smooth.

2. With an electric mixer, beat eggs until thick and light in color. Gradually add sugar and then vanilla extract, and beat about 8 minutes or until eggs reach the consistency of soft whipped cream.

3. Sprinkle flour over the surface of eggs, and gently fold in. Fold in chestnut mixture one-third at a time.

4. Lightly butter or spray the pan, and spread batter into it. Bake in the center of the oven 25–30 minutes or until a wooden toothpick inserted ½ inch from the center comes out clean.

5. Cool in pan on a rack. When the brownie has cooled, cut into quarters, and remove each quarter with a pancake turner. Pour Chocolate Glaze over each quarter, and spread with a spatula. When the glaze is firm, cut each quarter into 6 brownies.

CHOCOLATE GLAZE 2

> 2 *ounces semisweet chocolate*
> 2 *tablespoons boiling water*
> 2 *teaspoons cognac or rum*

1. Melt chocolate over hot water. Add the boiling water and the cognac or rum. Blend well.

2. Cool almost to room temperature and thick but not set.

CAPPUCCINO BROWNIES

A brandied chocolate-espresso brownie swirled with rum-brandy-flavored ricotta cheese filling touched with cinnamon. Let these sit at least 12 hours before serving to let the flavors mellow properly.

PREHEAT OVEN TO 350°F (340°F FOR GLASS)
8 × 8 METAL PAN

> *Rum-Brandy Ricotta Filling (below)*
> 5 *ounces good-quality semisweet chocolate*
> 6 *tablespoons unsalted butter*
> ¾ *cup stirred all-purpose flour*
> ¼ *teaspoon baking soda*
> ¼ *teaspoon salt*
> 2 *large eggs*
> 1 *teaspoon vanilla extract*
> ⅔ *cup granulated sugar*
> 2 *teaspoons brandy*

> 2 *teaspoons dry instant espresso powder*

1. Prepare Rum-Brandy Ricotta Filling, and set aside.

2. To prepare brownies, in a heavy small saucepan over very low heat or in a double boiler, melt the chocolate and butter together. When melted, mix until completely smooth; cool to room temperature.

3. Combine flour, baking soda, and salt in a small bowl or on wax paper.

4. In a food processor or with an electric mixer, beat eggs until light in color. Add vanilla extract and sugar, and beat 2 minutes. Then beat in brandy, espresso powder, cooled chocolate mixture, and flour mixture.

5. Lightly grease or spray pan. Pour two-thirds of the batter into it. Top evenly with the ricotta filling and then the remaining chocolate batter. To marbleize, cut through batter with a table knife, from side to side in a wide zigzag pattern.

6. Bake in the center of the oven 33–38 minutes or until a wooden toothpick inserted three-quarters from the edge of the pan comes out clean.

7. Completely cool brownies in pan on a rack, about 2 hours. Cover with alumi-

num foil and allow to stand at room temperature at least 12 hours before cutting into 20 or 24 brownies.

RUM-BRANDY RICOTTA FILLING

>   1 cup ricotta cheese, preferably
>   without gelatin
>   2 teaspoons light or amber rum
>   1 teaspoon brandy
>   ¾ teaspoon ground cinnamon
>   3 tablespoons unsalted butter at
>   room temperature
>   ⅓ cup granulated sugar
>   1 large egg
>   4 teaspoons cornstarch

1. Place the ricotta in a wire strainer, and hang it over a bowl for 1 hour to allow excess whey to drain off. Skipping this step will result in cakelike but soggy brownies. (The two can coexist.)

2. Remove ricotta from strainer, and place in the bowl of an electric mixer or food processor. Add remaining ingredients, and beat only until smooth.

❖

CHOCOLATE MOUSSE BROWNIES

These are feathery light but full of rich chocolate flavor. Serve them with lightly sweetened whipped cream, and decorate with Chocolate Leaves for a bit of unexpected elegance.

PREHEAT OVEN TO 375°F (360°F FOR GLASS)
9 × 13 METAL PAN

>   10 ounces good-quality semisweet
>   chocolate
>   ½ cup plus 1 tablespoon unsalted
>   butter cut into 5 pieces
>   1 tablespoon brandy or cognac
>   6 large eggs separated and left to
>   stand until room temperature
>   ¼ teaspoon salt
>   ½ cup granulated sugar
>   1½ teaspoons vanilla extract
>   2½ tablespoons sifted all-purpose
>   flour
>   whipped cream (optional)
>   Chocolate Leaves
>   (optional, page 157)

1. In a heavy medium saucepan over very low heat or a double boiler, melt chocolate and butter. Remove from heat, and stir until smooth and satiny. Stir in brandy or cognac. Cool to room temperature.

2. Prepare pan by lining it with parchment or foil according to directions on page 12. Grease the paper, or spray it well.

3. Beat egg whites and salt until opaque but not stiff. Gradually add ¼ cup sugar, reserving the rest, while beating whites to stiff peaks. Set aside.

4. Beat egg yolks until thick and light in color. Gradually add remaining sugar, and continue to beat until thick and light. Beat in the vanilla extract.

5. Pour the chocolate-butter mixture around the circumference of the beaten yolks, and fold in. Fold in one-third of the beaten egg whites. Fold in half of the flour, one-third of the egg whites, the remaining flour, and the remaining egg whites.

6. Bake in the center of the oven, 15–18 minutes or until barely set. A 1½-inch circle in the center will remain soft.

7. Cool completely on a rack. Chill before loosening cake from sides of pan and gently inverting onto a tray or baking sheet. Carefully peel away paper. Cut into 24–30 individual brownies and serve plain or, if you wish, with lightly sweetened whipped cream and Chocolate Leaves.

AMARETTI BROWNIES

Crushed Amaretti biscuits give these brownies their unique flavor.

PREHEAT OVEN TO 350°F (340°F FOR GLASS)
9 × 9 METAL PAN

16–17 *Amaretti biscuits*
 5 *ounces good-quality semisweet chocolate*
 ⅔ *cup unsalted butter at room temperature*
 1 *cup granulated sugar*
 4 *large eggs separated and left to stand until room temperature*
 ⅓ *cup stirred all-purpose flour*

1. Crush the Amaretti biscuits to crumbs in a blender or food processor. You should have ⅔ cup crumbs.

2. In a small pan within a larger pan over simmering water or in a double boiler, melt chocolate. Cool slightly.

3. In a food processor or with an electric mixer, beat butter until creamy. Gradually beat in sugar until fluffy. Add egg yolks, one at a time, beating each in well until mixture is fluffy. Blend in chocolate.

4. Add flour alternately with Amaretti crumbs.

5. In a clean bowl beat egg whites just until curved peaks will hold their shape

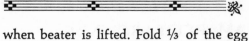
when beater is lifted. Fold ⅓ of the egg whites into the chocolate mixture. Fold chocolate into the remaining egg whites.

6. Grease the pan well, and pour batter into it.

7. Bake brownies in the center of the oven 45–50 minutes or until edges just begin to pull away from the pan and a wooden toothpick inserted 1 inch from the center comes out barely moist.

8. Cool in the pan on a rack overnight. After brownie has cooled a little, cover pan with foil.

9. Cut brownie into quarters, and remove each quarter with a pancake turner. Trim off the outer edges, and cut each quarter into 4 or 6 brownies. Store brownies wrapped airtight.

❖

WHITE CHOCOLATE– MARSHMALLOW BROWNIES

It might sound a bit corny to couple marshmallows with a sophisticated ingredient like white chocolate, but I urge you to fight off any tendencies toward food snobbery your palate might have to sample the delicate results of this marriage.

PREHEAT OVEN TO 350°F (340°F FOR GLASS)
8 × 8 METAL PAN

1½ cups mini-marshmallows
6 ounces white chocolate cut into pieces
3 tablespoons unsalted butter
2 large eggs
1 tablespoon granulated sugar
1 teaspoon vanilla extract
⅛ teaspoon salt
¼ teaspoon baking powder
½ cup sifted all-purpose flour
⅓ cup chopped almonds
20 almond slices

1. In a medium saucepan within a larger pan over simmering water or a double boiler, combine marshmallows, white chocolate, and butter. Cover the pan, and cook over low heat until ingredients are almost melted. Remove cover, and stir ingredients, still over the heat, until they are completely melted and smoothly mixed. Let cool slightly.

2. With an electric mixer, beat eggs until light in color. Add sugar, and beat an additional 3 minutes. Beat in vanilla extract, salt, baking powder, and slightly cooled chocolate mixture. Stir in flour and chopped nuts by hand.

3. Spray or lightly grease the pan. Spread batter into it, and smooth the top.

Place 4 evenly spaced rows of 5 un-blemished almond slices over the top of the batter to create 20 brownies each with an almond slice in its center.

4. Bake in the center of the oven about 25–30 minutes or until a wooden tooth-pick inserted 2½ inches from the edge of the pan comes out barely moist.

5. Cool in the pan on a rack 12 hours or overnight before cutting into 20 brownies.

GRASSHOPPER BROWNIES

Crème de cacao brownies with crème de menthe filling like the popular pie.

PREHEAT OVEN TO 350°F (340°F FOR GLASS)
9 × 9 METAL PAN

   8 ounces semisweet chocolate
   ⅔ cup unsalted butter
   6 large eggs
   ½ teaspoon vanilla extract
   ½ teaspoon salt
 1¼ cups granulated sugar
   1 cup sifted all-purpose flour
   2 tablespoons brandy
   2 tablespoons crème de cacao
      Crème de Menthe Filling (below)

1. In a heavy medium saucepan over very low heat or a double boiler, melt chocolate and butter. Blend well, and let cool to room temperature.

2. Lightly grease pans, or line with parchment (see page 12).

3. In a food processor or with an elec-tric mixer, combine eggs, vanilla extract, salt, and sugar; beat until blended. Add flour, and process 35 seconds or beat 1 minute. Beat in chocolate mixture and brandy.

4. Pour batter into pans, and bake, evenly spaced, about 20 minutes or until a wooden toothpick inserted ½ inch from the center comes out barely moist.

5. Cool layers in pans on racks for 2 hours. When cool, invert onto plates and gently peel away paper, if you used it. Prick layers evenly at 1½-inch intervals, and sprinkle each layer with 2 tablespoons of crème de cacao. Let brownie stand an hour, then chill for easier filling.

6. Spread Crème de Menthe Filling evenly on one brownie layer, and top it with the other, glossy side up. Press gently to even out filling. Chill until firm, 4–6 hours.

7. With a long thin, sharp knife, trim edges of the brownie, and cut into 4 strips. Turn strips on their sides, and cut each strip into 7 bars, wiping knife blade

with a damp towel when necessary. Serve brownies turned on their sides to show filling.

CREME DE MENTHE FILLING

    4 tablespoons unsalted butter at
        room temperature
    1 egg yolk
    ¾ cup powdered sugar
    3 teaspoons green crème de menthe

1. Combine butter, egg yolk, sugar, and crème de menthe. Blend with an electric mixer or fork until smooth and creamy.

2. If mixture seems too stiff, add a little more crème de menthe. Chill slightly before filling brownies.

CHOCOLATE ESPRESSO BROWNIES

A most continental brownie made with extra bittersweet Swiss chocolate, Italian espresso powder, and a coffee-brandy buttercream.

PREHEAT OVEN TO 350°F (340°F FOR GLASS)
9 × 13 METAL PAN

    6 ounces (2 3-ounce bars) extra
        bittersweet chocolate
    1⅓ cups stirred all-purpose flour
    ¾ teaspoon baking powder
    ¼ teaspoon salt
    4 teaspoons instant espresso
        powder
    4 large eggs
    1⅔ cups granulated sugar
    2 teaspoons vanilla extract
    ⅔ cup vegetable oil, carefully
        measured in a glass cup at eye
        level
        Coffee-Brandy Buttercream
        (below)
    ½ cup semisweet chocolate
        mini-morsels

1. In a small pan within a larger pan over simmering water or in a double boiler, melt the chocolate. Cool slightly.

2. Thoroughly combine flour, baking powder, salt, and espresso powder.

3. In a food processor or with an electric mixer, beat eggs until thick and light in color. Gradually add sugar while beating until well blended. Stir in vanilla extract, oil, and chocolate. Blend well. Stir in flour mixture.

4. Lightly grease, spray, or line the pan with paper (see page 12), and pour in batter. Bake in the center of the oven

25–30 minutes, until a wooden toothpick inserted ⅓ inch from the edge of the pan comes out dry.

5. Cool in the pan on a rack, then chill for easier frosting. If you have lined the baking pan, invert brownies onto a tray, peel away paper, and invert again before frosting with Coffee-Brandy Buttercream.

6. Sprinkle with chocolate mini-morsels.

7. Chill to set frosting before cutting into 28 or 32 brownies. (See cutting frosted brownies, page 13.)

COFFEE-BRANDY BUTTERCREAM

    2 egg yolks
    4 tablespoons (½ stick) unsalted
       butter
  2–4 teaspoons brandy or cognac
    1 teaspoon instant espresso powder
  1½ cups powdered sugar

1. In a small bowl with an electric mixer or fork, blend egg yolks, butter, and 2 teaspoons of brandy or cognac until smooth and fluffy. Add espresso and sugar, and beat until creamy.

2. Add additional brandy to taste but not enough to make frosting runny.

IRISH COFFEE BROWNIES

After the famous libation. A combination of coffee, chocolate, and Irish whiskey, topped with an Irish whiskey frosting.

PREHEAT OVEN TO 325°F
9 × 9 METAL PAN

    7 ounces semisweet chocolate
    6 tablespoons unsalted butter
   ⅔ cup sifted all-purpose flour
   ¼ teaspoons baking soda
   ¼ teaspoon salt
  2½ teaspoons instant coffee powder
    2 large eggs
   ½ cup granulated sugar
    2 tablespoons Irish whiskey
       Whiskey Cream (below)
       semisweet chocolate mini-morsels
       (optional)

1. In a heavy small pan over very low heat or in a double boiler, melt the chocolate and butter together. Remove from heat, stir until smooth, and let cool to room temperature.

2. Prepare pan by lining it with foil or parchment according to directions on page 12.

3. Combine sifted flour, baking soda, salt, and coffee powder. Mix well.

4. In a food processor or with an electric mixer, beat eggs until thick and

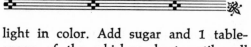
light in color. Add sugar and 1 table-spoon of the whiskey; beat until well blended.

5. Stir in chocolate mixture and then flour mixture just to blend.

6. Pour batter into prepared pan, and smooth top. Bake in the center of the oven 25–30 minutes (20–25 for glass pans) or until the top is shiny and a wooden toothpick inserted 1½ inches from the center of the cake comes out barely moist.

7. Cool in pan on a rack at least 2 hours. Loosen the edges of the cake from the pan, and invert onto a plate. Gently peel away paper.

8. Prick the cake at 1½-inch intervals with a wooden toothpick, and evenly pour the remaining whiskey over the surface one teaspoon at a time. Be sure each teaspoonful is absorbed before pouring on the next. Let stand 30 minutes. Cover and chill.

9. While cake is chilling, make Whiskey Buttercream (below). Spread buttercream smoothly over the surface of the cake. Sprinkle with chocolate mini-morsels, if desired, and chill again until topping is firm.

10. About an hour before serving, re-move brownie from the refrigerator, and cut into bars. (See cutting frosted brownies, page 13.) Serve brownies at room temperature.

WHISKEY CREAM

⅓ cup heavy cream, chilled
3 tablespoons unsalted butter at room temperature
½ cup powdered sugar
1½ teaspoons Irish whiskey

1. In a chilled bowl, with chilled beaters, beat whipping cream until fluffy; refrigerate.

2. Beat butter and sugar together until smooth. Blend in whiskey until smooth. Fold in half of the chilled whipped cream and then fold in the remaining cream.

—·5·—

NUT BROWNIES

❖

Why have a whole chapter on nuts in brownies? Why can't you just take a half cup or cupful of your favorite nuts and throw them into any recipe that calls for nuts? You can do that, of course, but if you're a true nut lover, you know that each type of nut has its own inherent qualities, and this fact makes it necessary to select a brownie that will complement and bring out the best of each nut.

The macadamia nut, with its rich, buttery flavor, is at its best in a light-textured German sweet brownie, while the very opposite is true for roasted whole almonds, whose faint bitterness is highlighted in the almost candylike chocolate brownie slabs of Brownie Almond Bark. Cashew nuts, with their delicate texture and subtle sweetness, are more at home in cakelike brownies, while the strong-flavored black walnuts are best in a dark, buttery, not-too-sweet concoction. Tender pecans are especially delightful in the Pecan Fudge Brownies, but don't overlook Rich and Buttery Pecan Brownies in "Unchocolate Brownies."

One of the many pleasures of writing this book was trying out the various possibilities, matching textures and flavor depths in the batter with the particular

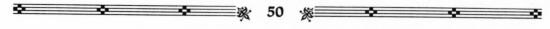
character of different nuts. I hope you will agree with my choices, but you can always experiment, too.

Although this is the nuttiest chapter in the book, you'll find other nut-filled recipes elsewhere, in particular in "Unchocolate Brownies," which has a variety of peanut, pecan, and almond brownie recipes, and "Healthful Brownies," which includes sunflower seeds along with other nutty variations.

BROWNIE ALMOND BARK

Almost like a candy. A thin, very choco-laty brownie filled with whole roasted almonds. And the quick-to-make batter can be mixed right in the chocolate pan.

PREHEAT OVEN TO 325°F
2 9 × 9 METAL PANS

   3 *ounces unsweetened chocolate*
   2 *ounces semisweet chocolate*
  ¾ *cup unsalted butter*
1¼ *cups granulated sugar*
  ¼ *teaspoon salt*
  2 *large eggs lightly beaten*
1½ *teaspoons vanilla extract*
 ⅔ *cup stirred all-purpose flour*
1¼ *cups roasted unsalted almonds*
      whole or very coarsely
      chopped

1. In a heavy medium pan over very low heat or in a double boiler, melt the chocolates and butter together. Mix thoroughly, and let cool slightly.

2. Stir the sugar and salt into the chocolate mixture, and then stir in the eggs; mix thoroughly. Stir in the vanilla extract and then flour just to mix.

3. Spray or lightly grease pans, and using half of the batter, pour a thin layer into each pan. Top with a layer of nuts and the remaining batter.

4. Bake in the center of the oven 16–24 minutes or until the top is dry and a wooden toothpick inserted 2 inches from the center comes out barely moist.

5. Cool in the pans on a rack about 6 hours or overnight. When cool, cut into bars about 1½ × 2½ inches, or break into random shapes.

MACADAMIA NUT BROWNIES

Cloudlike is the only way to describe the texture of this mixture of Baker's German's Sweet Chocolate and macadamia nuts in a frothy egg-whipped batter. The brownies are chocolaty, but the light texture and mild chocolate let the buttery taste of the nuts assert itself.

PREHEAT OVEN TO 375°F (360°F FOR GLASS)
9 × 9 METAL PAN

>   5   ounces Baker's German's Sweet
>   Chocolate, broken into pieces
>   (see chocolate measuring
>   notes, page 10)
>   5   tablespoons unsalted butter
>   3   large eggs at room temperature
>   ¼   teaspoon salt
>   ⅔   cup granulated sugar
>   1   teaspoon vanilla extract
>   ¼   cup stirred all-purpose flour
>   1   cup finely chopped macadamia
>   nuts

1. In a heavy saucepan over very low heat or in a double boiler, melt chocolate and butter together. Remove from heat, and stir together until smooth and satiny.

2. In the medium bowl of an electric mixer, beat eggs until light, foamy, and pale yellow. Add salt, and gradually add sugar about a teaspoon at a time while continuing to beat the eggs about 8 minutes or until they reach the consistency of whipped cream and a trail of egg will remain on the surface more than 15 seconds when the beaters are raised. Beat in vanilla extract.

3. Pour cooled chocolate mixture around the circumference of the eggs, and gently fold in, keeping mixture as airy as possible. Sprinkle 2 tablespoons of the flour over the batter, and gently fold in; repeat with the remaining flour. Fold in ⅔ cup of the nuts.

4. Spray or lightly butter pan, and pour batter into it. Sprinkle remaining nuts over the top. Bake in the center of the oven 27–35 minutes or until a wooden toothpick inserted 1 inch from the center comes out barely moist.

5. Cool in the pan on a rack at least 5 hours before cutting into 24 or 25 brownies. These brownies are best if not refrigerated. Store in the pan tightly covered with aluminum foil or in a tin.

❖

HAWAIIAN BROWNIES

Coconut and macadamia nuts in the same cloudlike batter again create a sort of macaroon brownie.

1. Follow directions for Macadamia Nut Brownies, substituting ½ cup chopped macadamia nuts and ½ cup sweetened shredded or flaked coconut in place of the 1 cup of nuts. Before baking, garnish the brownie with ¼ cup finely chopped macadamia nuts sprinkled over the top.

2. Bake and cool as directed in Macadamia Nut Brownies.

CASHEW NUT BROWNIES

A brown sugar brownie that enhances rather than overpowers the cashew nut flavor. If you wish, top it with Chocolate Chip Frosting (page 156), Small-Recipe Fudge Frosting (page 154), or Coffee-Brandy Buttercream (page 47), and sprinkle with additional cashews.

PREHEAT OVEN TO 350°F (340°F FOR GLASS)
9 × 9 METAL PAN

2 ounces unsweetened chocolate
1 cup sifted all-purpose flour
¼ teaspoon salt
¼ teaspoon baking powder
¼ teaspoon baking soda
⅔ cup butter or margarine at room temperature
1 cup packed light brown sugar
1 large egg
1 teaspoon vanilla extract
¼ cup light cream or milk
1¼ cups coarsely chopped roasted, unsalted cashews
frosting (optional)

1. In a small pan within a larger pan over simmering water or in a double boiler, melt chocolate. Remove from heat, and let cool to room temperature.

2. Combine flour, salt, baking powder, and soda; mix well.

3. In a food processor or with an electric mixer, cream the butter until fluffy. Add the sugar in thirds, and cream until light and ivory colored.

4. Add the egg, and beat until smooth. Stir in vanilla extract, cream or milk, and melted chocolate; mix well. Fold in flour mixture and 1 cup of the nuts.

5. Spray or lightly grease pan, and pour batter in; smooth top.

6. Bake in the center of the oven 25–

30 minutes or until a wooden toothpick inserted 1 inch from the center comes out barely moist.

7. Cool completely in the pan on a rack. When cool, frost and sprinkle with additional nuts. When frosting has set, cut into 20 or 24 brownies.

BLACK WALNUT BROWNIES

Pungent is the best word to describe these brownies. Dark, rich, buttery, and filled with the special flavor of black walnuts—an adult brownie.

PREHEAT OVEN TO 375°F (360°F FOR GLASS)
9 × 9 METAL PAN

   3 *ounces unsweetened chocolate*
 ⅔ *cup unsalted butter*
 ⅔ *cup sifted all-purpose flour*
 ¼ *teaspoon salt*
 ¼ *teaspoon baking powder*
  2 *large eggs*
  1 *cup granulated sugar*
1¼ *teaspoons vanilla extract*
  1 *cup black walnut pieces*
    Chocolate Glaze 2 (optional, page 40)

1. In a heavy small pan over very low heat or in a double boiler over simmering water, melt chocolate and butter. Remove from heat, and stir until thoroughly mixed. Let cool to room temperature.

2. Spray or lightly grease pan.

3. Thoroughly mix flour, salt, and baking powder.

4. In a food processor or with an electric mixer, beat eggs until light. Gradually add sugar, and beat until thoroughly mixed. Add vanilla extract and melted chocolate mixture; blend well. Fold in flour mixture and ⅔ cup of the nuts.

5. Spread batter in pan. If no glaze is to be used, chop remaining nuts fine, and sprinkle over batter. Otherwise, reserve to top glaze. Bake in the center of the oven 23–28 minutes or until a wooden toothpick inserted ½ inch from the center comes out barely moist.

6. Cool completely in the pan on a rack. Spread with chocolate glaze, if desired, and sprinkle with remaining nuts. Allow glaze to set before cutting into 20 or 24 brownies.

PECAN FUDGE BROWNIES

Some brownies, like some people, can never be too rich or too thin. These very buttery, very chocolaty, very rich, and thin but not too thin brownies are filled with loads of pecans.

PREHEAT OVEN TO 325°F
9 × 9 METAL PAN

> 3 ounces unsweetened chocolate
> ¾ cup unsalted butter
> 1¼ cups granulated sugar
> ¼ teaspoon salt
> 2 large eggs
> 1¼ teaspoons vanilla extract
> ¼ teaspoon baking powder
> ⅔ cup stirred all-purpose flour
> 1¼ cups pecan pieces (see page 7)

1. In a heavy medium saucepan over very low heat or in a double boiler, melt the chocolate and butter together. Mix thoroughly, and let cool slightly.
2. Stir sugar and salt into the chocolate mixture. Beat in eggs, one at a time. Stir in vanilla extract and baking powder. Stir in flour and nuts just to mix.
3. Spray, lightly grease, or line the pan with parchment (see page 12). Spread batter in the pan, and bake in the center of the oven about 35 minutes (30 for glass pan), or until a wooden toothpick

inserted three-quarters of the way from the edge of the pan comes out barely moist.

4. Cool in the pan on a rack 24 hours before cutting into 20 or 25 brownies. If you have lined the pan, loosen the edges of the brownie, invert onto a plate, and peel away paper. Invert again onto another plate, trim away dry edges, and cut into nice even quarters. Cut each quarter into 4 or 6 brownies.

EXTRA WALNUT BROWNIES

Rather than a brownie with some nuts, this brownie is many nut pieces coated with a dark, fudgy brownie. And there are even nuts on the top.

PREHEAT OVEN TO 325°F
9 × 9 METAL PAN

> 3 ounces unsweetened chocolate
> ¾ cup unsalted butter
> ⅔ cup stirred all-purpose flour
> ¼ teaspoon salt
> ¼ teaspoon baking powder
> 1¼ cups granulated sugar
> 2 large eggs

1¼ teaspoons vanilla extract
1⅔ cups chopped walnuts

1. In a heavy medium pan over very low heat or in a double boiler, melt chocolate and butter. Remove from heat, and stir until thoroughly mixed. Let cool to room temperature.
2. Spray or lightly grease pan.
3. Mix flour, salt, and baking powder thoroughly.
4. Stir sugar into cooled chocolate mixture. Beat in eggs one at a time. Mix in vanilla extract and flour mixture. Stir in all but ¼ cup nuts.
5. Spread batter in pan. Chop remaining ¼ cup nuts fine, and sprinkle evenly over batter.
6. Bake in the center of the oven 35–40 minutes (30 minutes for glass pan) or until wooden pick inserted 1 inch from the center comes out barely moist.
7. Cool completely in the pan on a rack, then chill several hours before cutting into 30 brownies.

MARZIPAN BROWNIES

Almond paste and chopped almonds go into this rich but not too sweet European-style brownie dessert.

PREHEAT OVEN TO 350°F (340°F FOR GLASS)
9 × 9 METAL PAN

> 4 *ounces unsweetened chocolate*
> 6 *tablespoons unsalted butter, at room temperature*
> 6 *tablespoons almond paste*
> 1¼ *teaspoons vanilla extract*
> ⅛ *teaspoon salt*
> 1⅓ *cups granulated sugar*
> 3 *large eggs*
> ¾ *cup stirred all-purpose flour*
> 1 *cup coarsely chopped raw almonds plus ¼ cup for optional garnish*
> *Chocolate Glaze 1 (optional, page 34)*

1. In a small pan within a larger pan over simmering water or a double boiler, melt the chocolate. Let cool to room temperature.
2. In the medium bowl of an electric mixer, cream butter until fluffy. Add almond paste, vanilla extract, salt, and sugar, and beat until light and creamy.
3. Add eggs one at a time, beating each one in well. Beat in cooled chocolate

on low speed. Stir in flour just until mixed. Fold in 1 cup of the nuts.

4. Spray or lightly butter pan, and pour in batter. Sprinkle top with the remaining nuts. Bake in the center of the oven 30–35 minutes or until a wooden toothpick inserted ½ inch from the center comes out barely moist.

5. Cool completely in the pan on a rack. If you wish, top brownies with Chocolate Glaze and then sprinkle with ¼ cup nuts before cutting into 20 or 24 brownies.

COCOA BROWNIES WITH PEANUT BUTTER–CHIP GLAZE

I like to use Dutch processed cocoa in this recipe. The topping is made by melting peanut butter chips on the warm brownies and spreading them to a glaze.

PREHEAT OVEN TO 350°F (340°F FOR GLASS)
9 × 13 METAL PAN

   1 cup sifted all-purpose flour
   ¾ cup unsweetened cocoa
   ½ teaspoon baking soda
   ¼ teaspoon salt

   ¾ cup butter at room temperature
   1½ cups packed light brown sugar
   3 large eggs
   1 teaspoon vanilla extract
   1 cup chopped unsalted roasted
        peanuts
   1 12-ounce package peanut butter
        chips

1. Combine flour, cocoa, baking soda, and salt; mix well.

2. In a food processor or with an electric mixer, cream butter and sugar together until light and fluffy. Add eggs, one at a time, beating each in well. Beat in vanilla extract. Stir in dry ingredients just to mix. Fold in ½ cup of the nuts.

3. Spray or lightly grease pan, and spread in batter evenly. Bake in the center of the oven about 30 minutes or until a wooden toothpick inserted ½ inch from the center comes out barely moist.

4. Remove from the oven to a rack; sprinkle with peanut butter chips. Let stand about 5 minutes to melt chips, and then spread melted chips evenly to form a glaze. Sprinkle on remaining nuts.

5. Cool completely before cutting into 28 or 32 brownies.

PEANUT BUTTER SWIRL BROWNIES

That favorite taste combination again. Semisweet and peanut butter batters swirl together in this brownie.

PREHEAT OVEN TO 325°F
9 × 9 METAL PAN

> 4 ounces semisweet chocolate
> 1⅓ cups stirred all-purpose flour
> ¼ teaspoon salt
> ¾ teaspoons baking powder
> ½ cup butter or margarine at room temperature
> 1½ cups granulated sugar
> 1½ teaspoons vanilla extract
> 3 large eggs
> 2 tablespoons milk
> 3 level tablespoons smooth peanut butter

1. In a small pan within a larger pan over simmering water or a double boiler, melt chocolate. Let cool slightly.

2. Combine flour, salt, and baking powder.

3. In a food processor or with an electric mixer, cream butter or margarine and sugar together until light and fluffy. Add vanilla extract and eggs, one at a time, mixing well after each. Blend in milk. Stir in flour mixture just to blend.

4. Remove one-third of the batter, about ⅞ of a cup, to a small bowl. Thoroughly blend in the peanut butter. Stir cooled chocolate into the remaining two-thirds of the batter.

5. Spray or lightly grease pan, and spread in about one-third of the chocolate batter. Drop remaining chocolate batter and peanut butter batter alternately, checkerboard fashion, onto the first layer of batter. Marbleize batters by swirling them gently with a table knife or spoon handle.

6. Bake in the center of the oven 40 to 45 minutes (40 for glass pan) or until a wooden toothpick inserted 1 inch from the center comes out barely moist.

7. Cool completely in the pan on a rack before cutting into 20 or 24 brownies.

PEANUT BUTTER– CHOCOLATE BROWNIES

The favorite combination of peanut butter and chocolate merge in this quick-to-prepare brownie.

PREHEAT OVEN TO 325°F
8 × 8 METAL PAN

2 ounces unsweetened chocolate
¼ cup butter or margarine at room
   temperature
¼ cup creamy peanut butter
1 cup packed light brown sugar
2 large eggs
1 teaspoon vanilla extract
½ cup sifted all-purpose flour
¾ cup chopped unsalted roasted
   peanuts

1. In a small pan within a larger pan over simmering water or a double boiler, melt chocolate. Let cool to room temperature.

2. In a food processor or with an electric mixer, cream butter or margarine, peanut butter, and sugar together until light and creamy. Beat in eggs one at a time, then beat in vanilla extract and melted chocolate. Fold in flour and ½ cup peanuts.

3. Spray or lightly grease pan, and pour in batter. Sprinkle with remaining peanuts. Bake in the center of the oven 30–35 minutes (25–30 for glass pans) or until brownie edges just begin to leave sides of the pan.

4. Cool completely in the pan on a rack before cutting into 16 or 20 brownies.

LAYERED COCONUT BROWNIE SUPREMES

A moist coconut layer tops this fudgy brownie.

PREHEAT OVEN TO 350°F (340°F FOR GLASS)
8 × 8 METAL PAN

1½ ounces unsweetened chocolate
⅓ cup vegetable shortening
⅔ cup sifted all-purpose flour
½ teaspoon baking powder
¼ teaspoon salt
2 large eggs
1 cup granulated sugar
½ teaspoon vanilla extract
⅓ cup sweetened, flaked coconut
¼ teaspoon almond extract

1. In a small pan within a larger pan over simmering water or a double boiler, melt chocolate. Let cool to room temperature.

2. Melt shortening over low heat.

3. In a bowl or on wax paper, combine flour, baking powder, and salt.

4. Beat eggs and sugar together. Beat in vanilla extract and melted shortening. Stir in flour mixture.

5. Put ½ cup of the batter in a small bowl, and mix in coconut and almond extract.

6. Add melted chocolate to remaining batter.

7. Lightly grease or spray pan, and spread chocolate batter in it. Drop coconut batter by the tablespoon over the surface of the chocolate batter, spreading carefully into a thin layer.

8. Bake in the center of the oven 25–30 minutes or until a wooden toothpick inserted 1 inch from the center comes out barely moist.

9. Cool completely in the pan on a rack before cutting into 20 or 24 brownies.

COCONUT-FILLED BROWNIES

A coconut-chocolate brownie with a spray of moist coconut garnishing the top.

PREHEAT OVEN TO 350°F (340°F FOR GLASS)
8 × 8 METAL PAN

> 2 *ounces unsweetened chocolate*
> 6 *tablespoons plus 2 teaspoons*
>   *butter or margarine*
> ⅔ *cup sifted all-purpose flour*
> ½ *teaspoon baking powder*
> ¼ *teaspoon salt*
> 2 *large eggs*
> 1 *cup plus 1 tablespoon granulated*
>   *sugar*
> 1 *teaspoon vanilla extract*
> 1⅓ *cups (3½ ounces) sweetened,*
>   *flaked, or shredded coconut*

1. In a heavy small pan over very low heat, or a double boiler, melt chocolate and 6 tablespoons of butter or margarine together. Let cool to room temperature.

2. Combine flour, baking powder, and salt.

3. Beat eggs until foamy, then beat in 1 cup of sugar and vanilla extract. Stir in chocolate mixture, flour mixture, and half of the coconut.

4. Lightly grease or spray pan, and spread in batter.

5. Melt remaining 2 teaspoons of butter or margarine. Add 1 tablespoon of sugar and the remaining coconut. Mix well, and sprinkle evenly over batter in pan.

6. Bake in the center of the oven 25–30 minutes or until a wooden toothpick inserted in the center comes out barely moist.

7. Cool completely in the pan on a rack. When cool, cut into 20 or 24 brownies.

—·6·—

FRUIT BROWNIES

❖

Fruit with chocolate has, on the whole, remained within the boundaries of European dessert and confectionery, except perhaps for chocolate-covered cherries and raisins and frozen bananas.

By now most Americans are acquainted with such enduring European classics as Sacher Torte, the dense chocolate cake glazed with apricot; semisweet chocolate Black Forest Cake, with its alternating layers of chocolate, cherries and whipped cream; or a variety of raspberry-chocolate gateaux and pavés that grace many good pastry carts. Such elegant specialties as poires belle Hélène, chocolate mousse with raspberry sauce, or gateau au Grand Marnier with bittersweet chocolate glaze are appearing on more menus, suggesting that there is a growing audience for the many possible combinations of fruit with chocolate that can be integrated into the brownie repertoire. Brimming with brandy-soaked dried fruits and nuts, Hungarian Brownies are among my favorites. Along similar lines are Black Forest Brownies with cherries and kirsch or Orange Brownies that use candied orange peel and Cointreau.

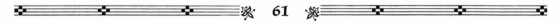
For more familiar tastes, and evry bit as appealing, try Apple Sauce Brownies flavored lightly with cinnamon, Moist and Chocolaty Date-Nut Brownies and Chocolate Raisin Jumble Brownies. Finally, both the Chocolate-Banana Brownies and the Banana-Chocolate Marbled Brownies will expand everyone's brownie horizons.

ORANGE BROWNIES

Pieces of candied orange peel flavor this not-too-sweet brownie.

PREHEAT OVEN TO 350°F (340°F FOR GLASS)
9 × 9 METAL PAN

  2 *teaspoons Cointreau (optional)*
 ½ *cup coarsely chopped candied*
     orange peel
  3 *ounces unsweetened chocolate*
 ¾ *cup sifted all-purpose flour*
 ¼ *teaspoon baking powder*
 ¼ *teaspoon salt*
 ½ *cup butter or margarine at room*
     temperature
  1 *cup packed golden brown sugar*
 ¼ *cup granulated sugar*
  2 *large eggs*
1¼ *teaspoons vanilla extract*

 ¾ *cup coarsely chopped almonds*
     (optional)
     Orange Buttercream
     (optional, page 33)

1. If you are using Cointreau, combine it with chopped orange peel. Mix well and let stand about 30 minutes.

2. In a small pan within a larger pan over simmering water or a double boiler, melt chocolate. Cool to room temperature.

3. Combine flour, baking powder, and salt.

4. With a food processor or an electric mixer, cream butter and sugars together until light and fluffy. Add eggs one at a time, beating each in well. Beat in vanilla extract and chocolate. Stir in flour mixture, chopped orange rind, and ½ cup of the nuts by hand.

5. Lightly grease or spray pan, and spread in batter. Sprinkle remaining nuts evenly over the top.

6. Bake in the center of the oven about 30 minutes or until a wooden toothpick inserted 1 inch from the center comes out barely moist.

7. Cool completely in the pan on a rack. When cool, cover the pan with foil, and allow the brownies to stand at least 24 hours. This will allow the flavors to mellow and the texture to develop correctly. Frost if you wish, and cut into 24–36 brownies.

BLACK FOREST BROWNIES

Fudgy squares of chocolate with kirsch-soaked cherries and nuts—what could be more German?

PREHEAT OVEN TO 350°F (340°F FOR GLASS)
9 × 9 METAL PAN

1¼ *cups chopped dried cherries*
3 *tablespoons kirsch*
½ *cup chopped walnuts*
6 *ounces Baker's German's Sweet Chocolate*
¼ *cup unsalted butter*

¾ *cup stirred all-purpose flour*
½ *teaspoon baking powder*
¼ *teaspoon salt*
3 *large eggs*
¾ *cup plus 2 tablespoons granulated sugar*
½ *teaspoon vanilla extract*

1. Combine chopped cherries and kirsch. Cover and marinate at least 3 hours or as long as 10 hours. Before beginning to bake, stir in nuts, and mix well.

2. In a heavy small saucepan over very low heat or a double boiler over simmering water, melt chocolate and butter together; blend well, and let cool slightly.

3. Combine flour, baking powder, and salt in a pan; mix well.

4. In a food processor or with an electric mixer, beat eggs until thick and light in color. Gradually beat in sugar, continuing to beat until mixture is thick. Stir in vanilla extract and chocolate mixture. Stir in flour mixture and cherries and nuts.

5. Spray or lightly grease baking pan and spread in batter. Bake in the center of the oven 30–35 minutes or until a wooden toothpick inserted 1 inch from the center comes barely moist.

6. Cool completely in the pan on a

rack. When cool, cover with foil, and allow it to stand overnight. Cut into 30 brownies.

APPLESAUCE BROWNIES

Another nice apple-chocolate combination in a slightly cakey brownie. Good with any chocolate frosting—Chocolate Chip (page 156), Small-Recipe Fudge (page 154), Dark Chocolate (page 155), or Spicy Chocolate Buttercream (page 131).

PREHEAT OVEN TO 350°F (340°F FOR GLASS)
9 × 9 METAL PAN

 2 *ounces unsweetened chocolate*
 1 *cup sifted all-purpose flour*
 ¼ *teaspoon salt*
 ½ *teaspoon ground cloves*
 ½ *teaspoon allspice*
1¼ *teaspoons ground cinnamon*
 ½ *teaspoon baking soda*
 ⅔ *cup butter or margarine at room temperature*
 1 *cup packed golden brown sugar*
 1 *large egg*
 1 *teaspoon vanilla extract*
 ⅓ *cup sweetened applesauce*
 1 *cup walnut or pecan pieces frosting (optional)*

1. In a small pan within a larger pan over simmering water or in a double boiler, melt chocolate. Remove from heat, and let cool to room temperature.

2. Combine the flour, salt, cloves, allspice, cinnamon, and baking soda; mix thoroughly.

3. In a food processor or with an electric mixer, cream the butter or margarine until fluffy. Add the sugar in thirds, and cream until light and ivory colored.

4. Add the egg, and beat until smooth. Stir in vanilla extract, apple sauce, and melted chocolate. Fold in flour mixture and nuts.

5. Spray or lightly grease pan, and pour in batter; smooth top.

6. Bake in the center of the oven 25–32 minutes or until a wooden toothpick inserted 1 inch from the center comes out barely moist.

7. Cool completely in the pan on a rack. When cool, frost if you wish, and sprinkle with extra nuts before cutting into 24 brownies.

HUNGARIAN BROWNIES

Reminiscent of Budapest Christmases, this mixture of brandied fruit and bitter-sweet chocolate is decidedly Old World. I used the packaged chopped dried mixed fruits containing apple, pear, peaches, apricots, raisins, and prunes. If you can't get this, substitute golden raisins or your own dried fruit mixture.

8 × 8 METAL PAN

MARINATED FRUIT MIX

⅓ cup quartered dried cherries
⅓ cup mixed dried fruits or golden raisins
½ cup chopped walnuts
⅓ cup chopped hazelnuts or almonds
2 tablespoons chopped dried orange peel or 2 teaspoons fresh minced orange zest
2½ tablespoons brandy or golden rum

BROWNIE

2½ ounces unsweetened chocolate
⅓ cup unsalted butter at room temperature
¼ teaspoon salt
⅔ cup granulated sugar
6 tablespoons packed golden brown sugar
3 level tablespoons light corn syrup
½ teaspoon vanilla extract
2 large eggs
¾ cup sifted all-purpose flour
Chocolate Glaze 1 (optional, page 34)

1. Combine all ingredients in Marinated Fruit Mix. Mix well, and marinate overnight.

2. Preheat oven to 375°F (360°F for glass pan). Line the pan with foil or parchment (see page 12).

3. In a small pan within a larger pan over simmering water or a double boiler, melt the chocolate. Let cool to room temperature.

4. With an electric mixer cream butter until fluffy. Gradually add salt and granulated sugar and then brown sugar; beat until light. Beat in corn syrup, vanilla extract, and eggs, one at a time, beating each in well.

5. Beat in melted chocolate. Stir in flour and Marinated Fruit. Mix by hand.

6. Spread batter in prepared pan, and bake in the center of the oven about 30 minutes or until the top is dry and a wooden toothpick inserted ¾ inch from the center comes out barely moist.

7. Cool in the pan on a rack about 1½ hours or until lukewarm. Invert cake onto a plate, and gently peel away paper. Invert cake again. When cake is completely cool, glaze if desired.

8. When glaze has set, cut into 25 or 36 brownies.

CHOCOLATE-APPLE BROWNIES

Spiced with a gentle hint of mace, a surprising and haunting flavor complement to chocolate and apples.

PREHEAT OVEN TO 350°F (340°F FOR GLASS)
9 × 9 METAL PAN

    2   ounces unsweetened chocolate
    1   cup sifted all-purpose flour
    ¼   teaspoon salt
    1   teaspoon ground cinnamon
    ½   teaspoon ground mace
    ½   teaspoon baking soda
    ⅔   cup butter or margarine at room
          temperature
    1   cup packed light brown sugar
    1   large egg
    1   teaspoon vanilla extract
    2   tablespoons milk

    1½ cups minced fresh apple
    1   cup walnut or pecan pieces
          Chocolate Chip Frosting (page
          156) or Spicy Chocolate
          Buttercream Frosting
          (page 131)
    ¼   cup finely chopped nuts (optional)

1. In a small pan within a larger pan over simmering water or a double boiler, melt chocolate. Remove from heat, and let cool to room temperature.

2. Combine the flour, salt, cinnamon, mace, and baking soda; mix thoroughly.

3. In a food processor or with an electric mixer, cream the butter until fluffy. Add the sugar in thirds, creaming until fluffy and ivory colored.

4. Add the egg, and beat until smooth. Stir in vanilla extract, milk, and melted chocolate; mix well. Fold in flour mixture, apples, and nuts.

5. Spray or lightly grease pan, and pour in batter; smooth top.

6. Bake in the center of the oven 30–35 minutes or until the top is dry and a wooden toothpick inserted 1 inch from the center comes out barely moist.

7. Cool completely on a rack. When cool, frost, and if you wish, sprinkle lightly with finely chopped nuts. Cut into 20 or 24 brownies.

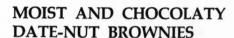

MOIST AND CHOCOLATY DATE-NUT BROWNIES

Chocolate and dates are a great flavor combination, and these moist brownies filled with chunks of dates and nuts create a texture that lives up to the taste.

PREHEAT OVEN TO 375°F (360°F FOR GLASS)
8 × 8 METAL PAN

2½	ounces unsweetened chocolate
⅓	cup butter or margarine at room temperature
¼	teaspoon salt
½	cup granulated sugar
⅔	cup packed golden brown sugar
3	tablespoons light corn syrup
2	large eggs
1	teaspoon vanilla extract
¾	cup sifted all-purpose flour
⅔	cup chopped pitted dates
⅔	cup walnut pieces

1. In a small pan within a larger pan over simmering water or a double boiler, melt chocolate. Let cool to room temperature.

2. In a food processor or with an electric mixer, cream butter, salt, and granulated sugar until light and fluffy. Add brown sugar, and beat until light. Beat in corn syrup and then eggs one at a time, beating each in well. Beat in vanilla

extract and chocolate. Stir in flour, dates, and nuts by hand just to mix.

3. Spray or lightly grease pan, and spread in batter. Bake in the center of the oven about 30 minutes or until the top is dry and a wooden toothpick inserted 1 inch from the center comes out barely moist.

4. Cool in the pan on a rack 24 hours before cutting into 24 or 30 brownies.

CHOCOLATE RAISIN JUMBLE BROWNIES

Use either golden or dark seedless raisins in this fruity chocolaty treat.

PREHEAT OVEN TO 350°F (340°F FOR GLASS)
9 × 9 METAL PAN

½	cup stirred all-purpose flour
½	cup unsweetened cocoa
⅛	teaspoon salt
1	teaspoon ground cinnamon
⅔	cup golden or dark raisins
½	cup semisweet or milk chocolate morsels
⅔	cup walnut pieces
½	cup butter or margarine at room temperature

1 cup granulated sugar
2 large eggs
1½ tablespoons light corn syrup
1 teaspoon vanilla extract
    powdered sugar (optional)

1. Combine flour, cocoa, salt, cinnamon, raisins, chocolate morsels, and nuts; mix well.

2. In a food processor or with an electric mixer, cream butter or margarine and sugar together until light and fluffy. Add eggs, one at a time, beating each in well. Beat in corn syrup and vanilla extract. Stir in dry ingredients just to mix.

3. Spray or lightly grease pan, and spread in batter.

4. Bake in the center of the oven 25–30 minutes or until a wooden toothpick inserted ½ inch from the center comes out barely moist.

5. Cool completely in the pan on a rack before cutting. Cut into 20 or 24 brownies. Sprinkle with powdered sugar just before serving, if desired.

CHOCOLATE-BANANA BROWNIES

PREHEAT OVEN TO 350°F (340°F FOR GLASS)
9 × 13 METAL PAN

1 cup (6 ounces) semisweet
    chocolate morsels
1 cup minus 2 tablespoons sifted
    all-purpose flour
⅔ cup granulated sugar
¼ teaspoon salt
¾ teaspoon ground cinnamon
½ teaspoon baking powder
¼ teaspoon baking soda
1 cup (about 2 medium) mashed
    ripe bananas
¼ cup butter or margarine at room
    temperature
1 large egg
½ teaspoon vanilla extract
1 cup chopped walnuts
    Chocolate Chip Frosting
    (page 156)

1. In a small pan within a larger pan over simmering water or a double boiler, melt chocolate morsels. Remove from heat, and stir until smooth.

2. Combine flour, sugar, salt, cinnamon, baking powder, and baking soda. Mix well.

3. In a food processor or with an

electric mixer, beat banana only until mashed. Add butter, and beat until smooth. Beat in egg and vanilla extract. Mix in melted chocolate until well blended. Mix in flour mixture and ⅔ cup of the nuts by hand until blended.

4. Spray or lightly grease pan, and spread in batter. Bake in the center of the oven 25–30 minutes or until a wooden toothpick inserted 1½ inches from the center comes out barely moist.

5. Cool in the pan on a rack at least 2 hours before frosting.

6. Frost with Chocolate Chip Frosting, and sprinkle with remaining nuts. Chill thoroughly.

7. With a long, thin, sharp knife cut into 28 or 35 brownies, wiping the blade clean with a damp towel when needed.

BANANA-CHOCOLATE MARBLED BROWNIES

PREHEAT OVEN TO 350°F (340°F FOR GLASS)
9 × 9 METAL PAN

1 cup (6 ounces) semisweet chocolate morsels

⅔ cup unsalted butter at room temperature
3 ripe bananas
1¼ cups stirred all-purpose flour
1 teaspoon salt
½ teaspoon ground cinnamon
½ teaspoon baking powder
¼ teaspoon baking soda
½ cup granulated sugar
1 large egg
½ cup chopped walnuts
Chocolate Chip Frosting (page 156) or Small-Recipe Fudge Frosting (page 154)

1. In a heavy saucepan over low heat or in a double boiler, melt chocolate pieces and 4 tablespoons of butter together. Mix thoroughly, and let cool slightly.

2. Mash the bananas, and measure off 1½ cups.

3. Combine flour, salt, cinnamon, baking powder, and baking soda; mix well.

4. Cream remaining butter and sugar until light. Beat in egg and then mashed banana. Blend in flour mixture.

5. Divide batter in half, and blend melted chocolate and nuts into one half the batter.

6. Spray or lightly grease pan. Drop chocolate batter and banana batter by alternate tablespoonfuls. Marbleize batters by swirling them together almost completely with a knife.

7. Bake in the center of the oven 25– 30 minutes or until the top is barely dry and the edges just begin to shrink from the sides of the pan.

8. Cool completely in the pan on a rack. Frost, and when frosting is set, cut into 20 brownies.

·7·

UNCHOCOLATE BROWNIES

What is a brownie if not chocolate? Certainly it would not be fair to overlook blond brownies, full of brown sugar butteriness and almost as well known as the original chocolate brownie. Once the fact that brownies can be light as well as dark is accepted, there's no reason not to move into the paler shades of tan, as with the delectable Unchocolate Almond Butter Squares, with that almond paste base, California Blondies, fragrant with citrus and almonds, or the Banana Nut and Chip Brownies.

After gathering brownie recipes from far and wide, I've come across quite a few unchocolate brownies. But where do you draw the line between cookies and brownies or, for that matter, between brownies and some cakes? A brownie is, after all, technically a bar cookie. The deciding factor is texture. A brownie must not be a cake, although some have leanings in that direction, and it must not be a crunchy cookie. Brownies are supposed to be chewy or somewhat fudgy textured, even when not fudgy colored.

Even if you are one of the people for whom treat and chocolate are synonymous, you shouldn't overlook this chapter. For while the dough base of

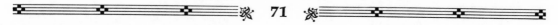
these brownies does not include chocolate, some are enhanced with chocolate in other ways. Banana Nut and Chip Brownies are good with a combination of nuts and semisweet morsels, or you can make them with nuts alone and frost them fudgily. The same suggestions work well with the Peanut Butter and Chocolate Chip Brownies, the Mandarin Orange Brownies, and James Beard's Blond Brownies.

Even though I'm among the most confirmed chocoholics, my favorites are the Unchocolate Almond Butter Squares and the California Blondies—both made without a trace of chocolate. (White chocolate is made from cocoa butter with the addition of emulsifiers, sugar, and vanilla. Many chocolate components are removed from it, so it is difficult to consider it a true chocolate. Nevertheless, it has a special deliciousness that springs from its chocolate source.)

NUTTY BLONDS

In spite of this whimsical name, these are serious brownies. A rich caramel batter is stuffed to the maximum with walnuts or pecans so that just a thin coating of buttery brownie surrounds each nut piece.

PREHEAT OVEN TO 350°F (340°F FOR GLASS)
8 × 8 METAL PAN

  ¼ cup butter
   1 cup packed golden brown sugar
  ¾ cup stirred all-purpose flour
   1 teaspoon baking powder
  ¼ teaspoon salt
   1 large egg
  ½ teaspoon vanilla extract
 1⅓ cups walnut or pecan pieces

1. In a medium saucepan over low heat, melt butter. Stir in sugar, and mix well. Let cool slightly.

2. Combine flour, baking powder, and salt, and set aside.

3. In a medium bowl, beat egg and vanilla extract together. Add brown sugar

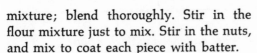
mixture; blend thoroughly. Stir in the flour mixture just to mix. Stir in the nuts, and mix to coat each piece with batter.

4. Spray or lightly grease pan, and spread in batter. Bake in the center of the oven about 25 minutes or until the top is slightly puffed and a wooden toothpick inserted 1 inch from the center comes out barely moist.

6. Cool in pan on a rack until barely warm. With a spatula, loosen edges of cake. Place a plate on top of the pan, and invert it, shaking slightly.

7. Cool cake completely before cutting into 20 or 24 brownies.

CALIFORNIA BLONDIES

The flavor of orange and lemon zest merge wonderfully with almonds in these moist squares. They are not Florida brownies, because the almonds are grown in California, and the author is a Californian.

PREHEAT OVEN TO 350°F (340°F FOR GLASS)
9 × 9 METAL PAN

    1¼ cups stirred all-purpose flour
    1¼ teaspoons baking powder
    ½   teaspoon salt
    ⅔   cup butter or margarine at room
         temperature
    ½   cup granulated sugar
    ⅔   cup packed golden brown sugar
    1   teaspoon vanilla extract
    2   teaspoons grated orange zest
    1   teaspoon grated lemon zest
    2   large eggs
    2   teaspoons milk
    1   cup chopped or slivered almonds

1. Combine flour, baking powder, and salt; mix well.

2. In a food processor or with an electric mixer, cream butter or margarine and granulated sugar until light and fluffy. Add brown sugar, and beat again until fluffy. Add vanilla extract and grated zests; mix well. Add eggs one at a time, beating each in well. Blend in milk. Stir in flour just to mix. Stir in nuts.

3. Spray or lightly grease baking pan, and spread in batter.

4. Bake in the center of the oven about 30 minutes, until a wooden toothpick inserted into the center comes out barely moist.

5. Cool completely in the pan on a rack. When cool, cover with foil, and let stand 8 hours or overnight. Cut into 20 or 24 blondies.

RICH AND BUTTERY PECAN BROWNIES

A thin caramel-like brownie filled to the brim with pecans and accented with a whisper of tart lemon. Wonderful for gift giving; wrapped airtight in foil, they will survive mailing beautifully.

PREHEAT OVEN TO 350°F (340°F FOR GLASS)
9 × 13 METAL PAN

> ½   cup unsalted butter
> 2   cups packed golden brown sugar
> 1½   cups stirred all-purpose flour
> 2   teaspoons baking powder
> ½   teaspoon salt
> 2   large eggs
> 1   teaspoon vanilla extract
> 1¼   teaspoons grated lemon zest
> 2⅔   cups pecan pieces

1. In a medium saucepan over low heat, melt butter. Stir in sugar, and mix well. Let cool slightly.

2. Combine flour, baking powder, and salt. Mix well.

3. In a medium bowl, beat eggs, vanilla extract, and lemon zest together. Add brown sugar mixture, and blend well. Stir in nuts, and mix to coat each piece with batter.

4. Lightly grease or spray pan, and spread in batter. Bake in the center of the oven about 30–35 minutes or until the top is slightly puffed and a wooden toothpick inserted 1 inch from the center comes out barely moist.

5. Cool completely in the pan on a rack before cutting into 40 small brownies with a long, thin, sharp knife.

BUTTERSCOTCH BROWNIES

PREHEAT OVEN TO 350°F (340°F FOR GLASS)
8 × 8 METAL PAN

> ½   cup butter or margarine
> 1   cup packed golden brown sugar
> 1   large egg
> ¼   teaspoon salt
> 1   teaspoon vanilla extract
> 1   cup sifted all-purpose flour
> ⅔   cup chopped walnuts or pecans

1. In a small pan, melt butter over low heat. Remove from heat, and stir in sugar. Transfer mixture to mixer bowl.

2. Beat butter mixture 1 minute, and then beat in egg, salt, and vanilla extract. Mix in flour and nuts.

3. Spray or lightly grease pan, and spread in batter. Bake in the center of the

oven 25–30 minutes or until a wooden toothpick inserted into the center comes out barely moist.

4. Cool completely in the pan on a rack before cutting into 20 brownies.

UNCHOCOLATE APPLE-NUT BROWNIES

This cinnamon apple-nut brownie may be made with or without chocolate. Make an unchocolate brownie, or simply add cocoa for a light chocolate flavor.

PREHEAT OVEN TO 350°F (340°F FOR GLASS)
9 × 13 METAL PAN

>   2 *cups sifted all-purpose flour*
>   2 *teaspoons baking powder*
> ¼ *teaspoon salt*
> ¼ *teaspoon ground allspice*
> 1¼ *teaspoons ground cinnamon*
> ⅔ *cup chopped walnuts*
> ⅔ *cup butter or margarine at room*
>   *temperature*
> 1½ *cups packed golden brown sugar*
>   2 *large eggs*
>   1 *teaspoon vanilla extract*
>   1 *cup chopped apple*
>   *powdered sugar*

1. Combine flour, baking powder, salt, allspice, cinnamon, and nuts; mix well.

2. In a food processor or with an electric mixer, cream butter or margarine and sugar together until light and fluffy. Add eggs, one at a time, beating each in well. Beat in vanilla extract. Stir in apple and then flour mixture just to mix.

3. Spray or lightly grease baking pan, and spread in batter. Bake in the center of the oven 25–35 minutes or until a wooden toothpick inserted ½ inch from the center comes out barely moist.

4. Cool completely in the pan on a rack. Before serving, dust lightly with powdered sugar, and cut into 32 brownies.

CHOCOLATE VARIATION

1. Stir ⅓ cup unsweetened cocoa into the flour mixture.

UNCHOCOLATE ALMOND BUTTER SQUARES

An elusively flavored, velvety textured *koekje*, the Dutch name given to small pieces of cake baked before the big cake

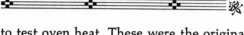
to test oven heat. These were the original cookies.

PREHEAT OVEN TO 350°F (340°F FOR GLASS)
9 × 9 METAL PAN

- ½ cup butter or margarine at room temperature
- 4 tablespoons almond paste
- 1 cup packed light brown sugar
- 1 large egg
- 1 tablespoon milk
- 1 teaspoon vanilla extract
- ¼ teaspoon salt
- 1⅓ cups sifted all-purpose flour
- ⅔ cup slivered almonds

1. With a food processor or electric mixer, cream butter, almond paste, and sugar together until light and creamy.

2. Beat in egg, milk, vanilla extract, and salt. Mix in flour by hand just to mix. Mix in all but ¼ cup nuts.

3. Spray or lightly grease pan, and spread in batter. Sprinkle with remaining nuts. Bake in the center of the oven 25–30 minutes or until a wooden toothpick inserted into the center comes out barely moist.

4. Cool completely in the pan on a rack before cutting into 20 or 24 brownies.

BANANA NUT AND CHIP BROWNIES

If you love banana nut bread, you will love these banana brownies with either semisweet or milk chocolate chips or the nut version with chocolate frosting.

PREHEAT OVEN TO 350°F (340°F FOR GLASS)
9 × 9 METAL PAN

- 1¼ cups stirred all-purpose flour
- ½ teaspoon baking powder
- ¼ teaspoon baking soda
- ½ teaspoon salt
- ¾ cup butter or margarine at room temperature
- ⅔ cup granulated sugar
- 1 teaspoon vanilla extract
- ½ teaspoon grated lemon zest
- 1 large egg
- 1½ cups mashed banana
- ¾ cup chopped walnuts
- ¾ cup semisweet or milk chocolate morsels plus ½ cup additional morsels for glaze (optional)

1. Combine flour, baking powder, baking soda, and salt; mix well.

2. In a food processor or with an electric mixer, cream butter or margarine and sugar together until light and fluffy. Add vanilla extract, lemon zest, and egg; beat until creamy.

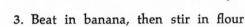
3. Beat in banana, then stir in flour mixture, nuts, and morsels just to mix.

4. Spray or lightly grease pan, and spread in batter. Bake in the center of the oven 30–37 minutes or until a wooden toothpick inserted ½ inch from the center comes out barely moist.

5. If you are glazing the brownies, sprinkle on a ½ cup of chocolate morsels immediately after removing brownie from the oven, and let stand 5 minutes. Spread chips evenly over brownies. If, you are not glazing the brownies, cool in the pan on a rack.

6. When the brownies are cool, cut into 20 or 24 bars with a long, thin, sharp knife.

FROSTED VARIATION

1. Omit chocolate morsels, and when brownies are cool, frost with Chocolate Chip Frosting (page 156) or Small-Recipe Fudge Frosting (page 154).

CLASSIC BLOND BROWNIES

Sometimes these are known as blondies. They differ slightly from a true butter-scotch brownie, which uses only brown sugar and is chewier. There are several ways to vary this basic recipe.

PREHEAT OVEN TO 350°F (340°F FOR GLASS)
9 × 9 METAL PAN

> 1¼ cups stirred all-purpose flour
> 1¼ teaspoons baking powder
> ½ teaspoon salt
> ⅔ cup butter or margarine at room temperature
> ½ cup granulated sugar
> ⅔ cup packed golden brown sugar
> 1 teaspoon vanilla extract
> 2 large eggs
> 2 teaspoons milk
> 1 cup walnut or pecan pieces

1. Combine flour, baking powder, and salt; mix well.

2. In a food processor or with an electric mixer, cream butter and granulated sugar together until light and fluffy. Add brown sugar, and beat again until fluffy. Add vanilla extract and eggs, one at a time, beating each in well. Blend in milk. Stir in flour mixture just to mix. Stir in nuts.

3. Spray or lightly grease baking pan. Spread batter into pan.

4. Bake in the center of the oven about 30 minutes or until a wooden toothpick

inserted into the center comes out barely moist.

5. Cool completely in the pan on a rack. When cool, cover with foil, and let stand 8 hours or overnight. Cut into 20 or 24 blondies.

BLONDIE VARIATIONS

1. Add 1¼ teaspoons ground cinnamon to the flour mixture.
2. Replace nuts with 1 cup semisweet chocolate morsels.
3. Replace nuts with ⅔ cup each nuts and morsels.
4. Add cinnamon to either Variation 2 or 3.

JAMES BEARD'S BLOND BROWNIES

These are the dean of American cooking's own white chocolate brownies. We have adapted the instructions to our format.

PREHEAT OVEN TO 325°F
8 × 10 OR 9 × 12 METAL PAN

  ½ cup unsalted butter
  5 ounces white chocolate
  2 cups granulated sugar
  2 large eggs
  1 teaspoon vanilla extract
  1 cup sifted all-purpose flour
  ½ teaspoon salt
  1 cup coarsely chopped walnuts,
      macadamia nuts, or pecans

1. In a medium pan over very low heat or in a double boiler over simmering water, melt butter and chocolate. Remove from heat, and stir well.

2. Stir in sugar and eggs one at a time, blending each in well. Beat in vanilla extract. Stir in the flour, salt, and nuts just to lightly mix.

3. Grease pan well, and spread in batter. Bake 35 minutes for smaller pan or 30 minutes for larger (5 minutes less for glass pan). Do not overbake, or brownies will lose their nice chewy texture.

5. Cool in the pan on a rack. With a greased knife, cut brownies into 24 bars while still slightly warm.

MANDARIN ORANGE BROWNIES

An orange brownie complemented by semisweet or extra bittersweet chocolate and almonds. A memorable combination.

PREHEAT OVEN TO 350°F (340°F FOR GLASS)
9 × 9 METAL PAN

1¼   cups stirred all-purpose flour
1¼   teaspoons baking powder
½   teaspoon salt
⅔   cup butter at room temperature
⅔   cup granulated sugar
½   cup packed golden or light brown
        sugar
1   teaspoon vanilla extract
4½   teaspoons grated orange zest
2   teaspoons Cointreau or orange
        juice concentrate
2   large eggs
⅔   cup chopped blanched almonds
¾   cup semisweet chocolate morsels
        or 5 ounces extra bittersweet
        chocolate broken into tiny
        pieces

1.   Combine flour, baking powder, and salt; mix well.
2.   In a food processor or with an electric mixer, cream butter and granulated sugar together until light and fluffy. Add brown sugar, and beat again until fluffy.

Add vanilla extract and orange zest; mix well. Beat in Cointreau or orange juice concentrate. Add eggs, one at a time, beating each in well. Stir in flour mixture just to blend. Mix in almonds and morsels or bittersweet chocolate pieces.
3.   Spray or lightly grease baking pan, and spread in batter.
4.   Bake in the center of the oven about 35 minutes or until a wooden toothpick inserted into center comes out barely moist.
5.   Cool completely in the pan on a rack. When cool, cover with foil and let stand 8 hours or overnight. Cut into 20 or 24 brownies.

❖

PEANUT BUTTER–CHOCOLATE CHIP BROWNIES

A peanut butter (not chocolate) brownie with chocolate chips and a chocolate glaze. Use either semisweet or milk chocolate morsels.

PREHEAT OVEN TO 350°F (340°F FOR GLASS)
9 × 13 METAL PAN

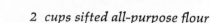 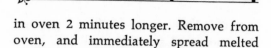
2 cups sifted all-purpose flour
1¾ teaspoons baking powder
¼ teaspoon salt
⅓ cup creamy peanut butter at room temperature
1 cup butter or margarine, at room temperature
1 cup granulated sugar
¾ cup packed golden brown sugar
1 teaspoon vanilla extract
3 large eggs
9 ounces (1½ cups) semisweet or milk chocolate morsels

1. Combine flour, baking powder, and salt.

2. In a food processor or with an electric mixer, beat peanut butter and butter or margarine until creamy. Beat in sugars and vanilla extract. Add eggs, one at a time, beating each in well.

3. Gradually beat in flour mixture just until well combined. Fold in 1 cup of the morsels.

4. Spray or lightly grease pan, and spread in batter evenly. Bake in the center of the oven 35–40 minutes or until the top is dry and a wooden toothpick inserted into the center comes out barely moist.

5. Sprinkle brownies with remaining ½ cup of chocolate morsels, and leave in oven 2 minutes longer. Remove from oven, and immediately spread melted chocolate over entire surface of cake.

6. Cool completely in pan on a rack before cutting into 32 brownies.

❖

GRANOLA BUTTERSCOTCH SQUARES

Granola gives a nutlike quality without any nuts. Try to get a granola that's not too sweet, or the sweetness will be overbearing.

PREHEAT OVEN TO 350°F (325°F FOR GLASS)
8 × 8 METAL PAN

¼ cup butter
1 cup packed golden brown sugar
¾ cup stirred all-purpose flour
1 teaspoon baking powder
1 teaspoon ground cinnamon
¼ teaspoon salt
1 large egg
½ teaspoon vanilla extract
¾ cup granola

1. In a medium saucepan over low heat, melt butter. Stir in sugar, and mix well; let cool slightly.

2. Combine flour, baking powder, cinnamon, and salt. Mix well.

3. In a medium bowl, beat egg and vanilla extract together. Add brown sugar mixture; blend thoroughly. Stir in flour mixture just to mix. Stir in granola, and mix to thoroughly distribute granola.

4. Spray or lightly grease pan, and spread in batter. Bake in the center of the oven about 25 minutes or until the top is slightly puffed and a wooden toothpick inserted 1 inch from the center comes out barely moist.

5. Cool in the pan on a rack until barely warm. With a spatula, loosen edges of cake. Place a plate on top of pan, and invert it, shaking slightly.

6. Cool completely before cutting into 20 or 24 brownies.

GRANOLA VARIATIONS

1. Add ⅔ cup dark or golden raisins to the batter with the granola.

2. Mix in ⅔ cup sliced pitted dates with the granola.

—·8·—

HEALTHFUL BROWNIES

❖

Admittedly, not all brownies have much going for them as a food, other than tasting wonderful—and often that's enough. Much as I love rich and seductive brownies, a continuous diet of such extravaganzas sometimes wears thin, and then it's the simpler, heartier tastes and textures that appeal. Each of the brownies in this chapter has a special place in my repertoire. Try Carob-Apple Whole Wheat Brownies, fruity, cinnamon flavored, and filled with walnut chunks—the perfect accompaniment to afternoon tea or even morning coffee. Honey, whole wheat flour, and chewy dried fruits make a really substantial snack or dessert in the Honey-Carob Brownies. Another variation of these brownies uses a mixture of freshly roasted sunflower seeds and walnuts in place of the fruit. Maida Heatter's dazzling Whole Wheat Brownies delight with raisins, whole wheat flour, spices, and—yes—chocolate. You may echo her husband's comment the first time she served them to him: "I know these are brownies, but what did you do? These have more 'oomph.'"

Depending on their ingredients, brownies can contribute to our nutrition instead of just being dietary frills. Wheat germ, for example, one of the most

nutritious foods, adds a nutlike richness and delicious texture when judiciously used; adding some to just any cookie or brownie recipe may not produce satisfactory results, but when used in the right proportion, such wonders as Wheat Germ Butterscotch Brownies are produced. Chewy and flourless, this brownie metamorphoses into a macaroonlike bar filled with vanilla caramel flavor. Eyebrows may raise at the thought of Zucchini Brownies or Chocolate Potato Brownies, but why not? Remember how surprised people were at the debut of carrot cake, now a national favorite?

In matters of healthful cooking, the honey-sugar question is often raised. While there is not a significant nutritional difference between the two, some cooks prefer honey not only for its trace nutrients and enzymes but for the flavor and moisture it contributes to baked goods.

Carob is another ingredient frequently found in healthful sweets. Though often considered a chocolate substitute, carob has a distinct taste of its own. Because carob has no caffeine and is lower in oil and higher in protein than chocolate, some people feel more virtuous when eating sweets made with it. Note, however, that carob has a fair amount of tannin.

There is also something to be said for the somewhat more healthful brownie. No purist, I like merging the best of both brownie worlds in my favorite, Chocolate Wheat Germ Brownies. This delicious confection satisfies my chocolate cravings but consoles me with the knowledge that something so good has more than just empty calories. Remember that chocolate contains small amounts of iron and calcium; furthermore, its protein, when mixed with nuts or wheat germ, becomes more nutritionally useful.

CHOCOLATE WHEAT GERM BROWNIES

Only a semidecadent brownie.

PREHEAT OVEN TO 350°F (340°F FOR GLASS)
9 × 13 METAL PAN

- 4 ounces unsweetened chocolate
- ¾ cup butter
- 2 cups turbinado or granulated sugar
- ½ cup stirred whole wheat flour
- ⅔ cup unbleached all-purpose flour
- 1 cup wheat germ
- ½ teaspoon salt
- 2 teaspoons baking powder
- 3 large eggs lightly beaten
- 1½ teaspoons vanilla extract
- 1½ cups broken walnuts or pecans

1. In a heavy medium pan over very low heat or a double boiler, melt chocolate and butter together. Remove from heat, and blend together thoroughly. Mix in sugar.

2. Combine flours, wheat germ, salt, and baking powder in a bowl, and mix well.

3. Add eggs and vanilla extract to chocolate mixture, and blend well. Stir in flour mixture and nuts just to mix.

4. Spray or lightly grease pan, and spread in batter. Bake in the center of the oven 27–30 minutes, until a wooden toothpick inserted 1 inch from the center comes out barely moist.

5. Cool 2 hours in the pan on a rack before cutting into 32 brownies.

HONEY-CAROB BROWNIES

A delicious nutritious snack with many virtues, this brownie is made with whole wheat pastry flour, carob powder, and honey.

PREHEAT OVEN TO 350°F (340°F FOR GLASS)
9 × 9 METAL PAN

- 1 cup sifted whole wheat pastry flour (not regular whole wheat flour)
- 6 tablespoons carob powder
- 1 teaspoon baking powder
- ¼ teaspoon salt
- ½ cup butter or margarine
- 1¼ cups honey
- 2 large eggs, beaten
- 1¼ teaspoons vanilla extract
- ⅔ cup broken walnuts

1. Combine flour, carob powder, baking powder, and salt. Mix well.

2. In a medium saucepan melt butter or margarine over low heat. Add honey, and mix well. Remove from heat, and let cool slightly.

3. Beat in eggs and vanilla extract. Stir in flour mixture and nuts.

4. Spray or lightly grease pan, spread in batter. Bake in the center of the oven about 45 minutes or until a wooden toothpick inserted ½ inch from the center comes out barely moist.

5. Cool 2 hours in the pan on a rack before cutting into 20 brownies.

HONEY CAROB VARIATIONS

1. Replace ⅔ cup walnuts with ⅔ cup chopped mixed dried fruit and ½ cup chopped walnuts.

2. Replace ⅔ cup broken walnuts with ⅓ cup unsalted roasted sunflower seeds and ½ cup chopped walnuts.

DOUBLE CHOCOLATE WHOLE WHEAT BROWNIES

The chocolatiest whole wheat brownies. A mixture or freshly roasted unsalted sunflower seeds and walnuts is nice in these.

PREHEAT OVEN TO 350°F (340°F FOR GLASS)
8 × 8 METAL PAN

  2 *ounces unsweetened chocolate*
  5 *tablespoons butter or margarine*
 ⅓ *cup unsweetened cocoa*
 ¾ *cup stirred whole wheat flour*
 ½ *teaspoon baking soda*
 ⅛ *teaspoon salt*
  1 *cup turbinado or granulated sugar*
  2 *large eggs*
 ¼ *cup milk*
1½ *teaspoons vanilla extract*
 ⅔ *cup chopped walnuts or ¼ cup unsalted roasted sunflower seeds and ½ cup chopped walnuts (optional)*

1. In a heavy small pan over very low heat or in a double boiler, melt chocolate and butter or margarine together; let cool to room temperature.

2. Combine cocoa, flour, baking soda, and salt.

3. Beat sugar and eggs together. Beat in milk and vanilla extract. Mix in chocolate mixture and then flour mixture. Stir in nuts and seeds, if using them.

4. Spray or lightly grease pan, and spread in batter. Bake in the center of

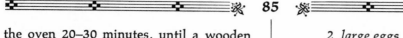
the oven 20–30 minutes, until a wooden toothpick inserted ½ inch from the center comes out barely moist.

5. Cool completely in the pan on a rack before cutting into 16 or 20 brownies.

MAIDA HEATTER'S WHOLE WHEAT BROWNIES

These are from *Maida Heatter's Book of Great Chocolate Desserts*. She attributes their unusual deliciousness to the use of spices, brown sugar, raisins, and, of course, whole wheat flour.

PREHEAT OVEN TO 350°F
8 × 8 METAL PAN

   2 ounces unsweetened chocolate
   ½ cup plus 2 tablespoons
       all-purpose whole wheat flour
   ½ teaspoon ground cinnamon
   ½ teaspoon ground ginger
   ½ teaspoon ground allspice
   ½ cup (1 stick) unsalted butter at
       room temperature
   ½ (scant) teaspoon salt
   ½ teaspoon vanilla extract
   1 cup packed light or dark brown
       sugar

   2 large eggs
   1 generous cup walnuts, broken
       into medium-sized pieces
   ½ cup raisins

1. Adjust oven rack ⅓ up from bottom of oven before preheating oven.

2. Prepare cake pan by lining it with aluminum foil as directed on page 12.

3. In a small pan within another pan over simmering water or a double boiler, melt chocolate. Cool slightly.

4. Put about 1 cup of flour in a strainer, over a bowl. Stir to strain. When you are finished, add any remaining bran in the strainer to the bowl. Stir and measure out ½ cup and 2 tablespoons of flour. Combine measured flour with the cinnamon, ginger, and allspice; mix well.

5. In the small bowl of an electric mixer, cream the butter. Add the salt, vanilla extract, and sugar. Beat until well mixed. Add eggs one at a time, beating only until smooth after each one. Add the chocolate, and beat only until smooth. Add the flour mixture, beating only until incorporated. Stir in the walnuts and raisins.

6. Turn batter into the prepared pan, and spread it to make an even layer.

7. Bake about 30 minutes or until a toothpick gently inserted in the center of

the cake comes out barely clean and dry. There may be a few specks of chocolate clinging to the toothpick. Do not over-bake.

8. Cool in the pan on a rack to room temperature.

9. Cover the pan with a rack, and invert pan and rack. Remove the pan and aluminum foil. Cover with another rack, and invert again, leaving brownie right side up.

10. Freezing brownie until quite firm makes it easier to cut. Use a long, sharp or, preferably, serrated knife, on a cutting board, to cut brownies into 16 squares.

11. Store cut brownies on a tray tightly covered with plastic wrap, or individually wrapped.

FUDGY OATMEAL–
WHEAT GERM BROWNIES

PREHEAT OVEN TO 350°F (340°F FOR GLASS)
8 × 8 METAL PAN

 1 *cup (6 ounces) carob or*
   semisweet chocolate morsels
 5 *tablespoons butter or margarine*

 ¾ *cup plus 2 tablespoons quick-*
   cooking oatmeal*
 ¼ *cup toasted wheat germ*
 ⅓ *cup nonfat dry milk*
 ½ *teaspoon baking powder*
 ½ *teaspoon salt*
 ½ *cup chopped walnuts*
 2 *large eggs*
 ½ *cup turbinado sugar or ¼ cup*
   granulated and ¼ cup packed
   golden brown sugar
 1 *teaspoon vanilla extract*

1. In a saucepan over very low heat, melt carob or chocolate morsels and butter; let cool slightly.

2. While carob or chocolate is melting, combine oatmeal, wheat germ, nonfat dry milk, baking powder, salt, and walnuts. Mix well.

3. In the medium mixing bowl of an electric mixer or in a food processor, beat eggs until light, then beat in sugar and vanilla extract. Stir in chocolate mixture, blending well. Stir in oat mixture just until well blended; do not overmix.

4. Grease or spray a pan, and spoon in

* For extra fudgy brownies use only ¾ cup oatmeal. Be sure to chill brownies thoroughly before cutting.

batter, spreading evenly. Bake in the center of the oven 20–25 minutes or until the top is crisp and the edges are firm. An area in the center roughly 2 inches square will still be soft.

5. Cool brownies in the pan on a rack, then cover with foil and chill overnight. Cut into 16 squares while chilled.

WHEAT GERM BUTTERSCOTCH BROWNIES

Moist and chewy squares with a subtle nutlike flavor. These interesting brownies are flourless.

PREHEAT OVEN TO 350°F (340°F FOR GLASS)
8 × 8 METAL PAN

- ¼ cup vegetable oil
- 1 tablespoon light molasses
- 2 large eggs
- ¾ cup plus 2 tablespoons packed golden brown sugar
- 1 teaspoon vanilla extract
- ⅔ cup nonfat dry milk
- ½ teaspoon baking powder
- 1 cup toasted wheat germ
- ½ cup chopped walnuts

1. In a food processor or with an electric mixer, combine oil, molasses, eggs, sugar, and vanilla extract; blend until smooth.

2. Blend dried milk, baking powder, and wheat germ in a bowl; mix thoroughly, and blend into batter. Stir in nuts.

3. Spray or lightly grease pan, and spread in batter.

4. Bake in the center of the oven about 30 minutes or until the top is dry.

5. Cool completely in the pan on a rack before cutting into 20 or 25 brownies.

JEANNIE KIM'S GRANOLA-NUT BUTTERSCOTCH BROWNIES

Jeannie Kim, my helper and recipe tester, came up with this idea.

1. Follow steps 1–2 of Wheat Germ Butterscotch Brownies. After adding wheat germ, stir in ¾ cup granola.

2. Bake in a 9 × 9 pan. Reduce cooking time to about 25 minutes.

CAROB-APPLE WHOLE WHEAT BROWNIES

This fiber-rich brownie, flavored with apple, spices, and carob, is as delicious as it is healthful.

PREHEAT OVEN TO 350°F (340°F FOR GLASS)
9 × 13 METAL PAN

1⅓	cups stirred whole wheat flour
⅔	cup unbleached all-purpose flour
⅓	cup unsweetened carob powder
1	teaspoon ground cinnamon
½	teaspoon ground mace
2	teaspoons baking powder
¾	cup chopped walnuts
¾	cups butter at room temperature
1½	cups packed golden brown or turbinado sugar
2	large eggs
1	teaspoon vanilla extract
1	cup chopped, fresh apple
2	tablespoons toasted wheat germ
⅓	cup carob morsels (optional)

1. Mix flours, carob powder, cinnamon, mace, baking powder, and nuts; mix well.

2. In a food processor or with an electric mixer, cream butter and sugar until light and fluffy. Add eggs, one at a time, beating each in well. Beat in vanilla extract. Stir in apples and then dry ingredients just to blend.

3. Spray or lightly grease baking pan. Spread in batter, and sprinkle on wheat germ over the surface of the batter. Bake in the center of the oven 27–35 minutes or until a wooden toothpick inserted 1 inch from the center comes out barely moist.

4. Remove from oven, and let cool 5 minutes. Sprinkle on carob morsels.

5. Cool completely in the pan on a rack before cutting into 32 brownies.

❖

POWER-PACKED CAROB BROWNIES

This brownie is filled with all kinds of nutritious ingredients and is a good mixture of complementary proteins, making it a nourishing meal in a bar.

PREHEAT OVEN TO 350°F (340°F FOR GLASS)
9 × 9 METAL PAN

1	cup toasted wheat germ
⅔	cup nonfat dry milk
½	teaspoon baking powder
⅛	teaspoon salt
6	tablespoons unsweetened carob powder
¼	cup vegetable oil

1 tablespoon light molasses
1¼ cups packed golden brown or
   turbinado sugar
2 teaspoons vanilla extract
2 large eggs
⅔ cup broken walnuts or pecans

1. Combine wheat germ, dry milk, baking powder, salt, and carob powder, and mix well.

2. In a food processor or with an electric mixer, blend oil, molasses, sugar, and vanilla extract; beat until light. Add eggs, one at a time, beating each in well. Stir in dry ingredients just to mix. Stir in nuts by hand.

4. Spray or lightly grease baking pan, and spread in batter.

5. Bake in the center of the oven 25–30 minutes or until a wooden toothpick inserted 2 inches from the center comes out clean.

6. Cool 15 minutes. Turn out of pan, and cool about 1 hour before cutting into 20 bars.

CAROB CHIP BARS

A carob batter with chocolate chips and nuts throughout.

PREHEAT OVEN TO 350°F (340°F FOR GLASS)
9 × 9 METAL PAN

½ cup butter at room temperature
½ cup carob nuggets
½ cup honey
¼ cup packed golden brown sugar
1 large egg
2 tablespoons milk
1 teaspoon vanilla extract
¼ teaspoon salt
1 teaspoon baking powder
⅔ cup stirred whole wheat flour
¼ cup unbleached all-purpose flour
⅔ cup chopped walnuts
⅔ cup carob nuggets

1. Combine butter and ½ cup carob nuggets in a heavy saucepan. Cook over very low heat until both are melted. Mix well.

2. Add honey and sugar, and stir together until completely blended. Remove from heat, and let cool almost to room temperature.

3. Beat in egg, milk, vanilla extract, and salt. Sprinkle baking powder over the batter, and blend in. Mix in flours

and all but 3 tablespoons of the nuts. Stir in carob nuggets.

4. Spray or lightly grease a pan, and spread in batter. Finely chop remaining nuts, and sprinkle over the surface of the batter.

5. Bake in the center of the oven 25–30 minutes or until a wooden toothpick inserted 1 inch from the center comes out barely moist.

6. Cool completely in the pan on a rack before cutting into 24 brownies.

CHOCOLATE POTATO BROWNIES

Potatoes show up in many German and Viennese home-style desserts, and they are right in their element in these chocolaty brownies. Be sure to use mashed potato without added milk. Russet potatoes are the best.

PREHEAT OVEN TO 350°F (340°F FOR GLASS)
9 × 9 METAL PAN

    2 ounces unsweetened chocolate
    2 ounces semisweet chocolate
    1/3 cup butter or margarine

    1 tablespoon vegetable shortening
    1 cup sifted unbleached all-purpose
       flour or 1/2 cup whole wheat
       and 1/2 cup unbleached
       all-purpose flour
    1/2 teaspoon baking soda
    1/2 teaspoon baking powder
    1/4 teaspoon salt
    2 large eggs
    1 1/4 cups granulated sugar
    1 teaspoon vanilla extract
    1/2 cup cold mashed potatoes

1. In a heavy small pan over very low heat or in a double boiler, melt the chocolates, butter or margarine, and shortening together. Let cool slightly.

2. Combine flour, baking soda, baking powder, and salt; mix well.

3. In a food processor, with an electric mixer, or by hand, beat eggs, sugar, and vanilla extract together. Beat in mashed potatoes and then the chocolate mixture. Stir in the flour mixture just to blend.

4. Spray or lightly grease baking pan, and spread in batter.

5. Bake in the center of the oven 22–27 minutes, until a wooden toothpick inserted 1 inch from the center comes out barely moist.

6. Cool completely in the pan on a rack before cutting into 20 brownies.

ZUCCHINI BROWNIES

Zucchini bread was the rage for a while, so maybe zucchini brownies will be next.

PREHEAT OVEN TO 350°F (340°F FOR GLASS)
9 × 9 METAL PAN

<blockquote>

1   *cup finely chopped (not shredded) zucchini*

½   *teaspoon salt*

⅓   *cup butter, at room temperature*

1   *cup packed golden brown or turbinado sugar*

1   *large egg*

1½   *teaspoons vanilla extract*

1   *cup stirred unbleached, all-purpose flour or ½ cup each white and whole wheat flour*

⅓   *cup unsweetened carob powder or unsweetened cocoa*

¼   *teaspoon baking powder*

1½   *teaspoons ground cinnamon*

¼   *teaspoon ground nutmeg*

¾   *cup chopped nuts*
    powdered sugar (optional)
    Small-Recipe Fudge Frosting (page 154) or Chocolate Chip Frosting (page 156)

</blockquote>

1. Place zucchini in a colander, sprinkle with salt, and let stand 20 minutes. Gently blot dry with paper towels.

2. In a food processor or with an electric mixer, beat butter and sugar until fluffy. Add egg and vanilla extract, and beat until creamy.

3. Combine flour, carob or cocoa, baking powder, cinnamon, and nutmeg in a bowl. Blend well, then stir into butter mixture just until blended. Stir in nuts and zucchini by hand.

4. Spray or lightly grease pan, and spread in batter.

5. Bake in the center of the oven 25–30 minutes or until a wooden toothpick inserted 1 inch from the center comes out barely moist.

6. Cool completely in the pan on a rack. If desired, sprinkle with powdered sugar right before serving or frost. Cut into 20 or 25 brownies.

❖

JUEL ANDERSEN'S BAKED TOFU FUDGE BROWNIES

Juel Andersen has written many books about tofu and its use. This recipe comes from *Juel Andersen's Tofu Kitchen*. The ingredient okara is soybean bran, the

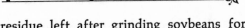
residue left after grinding soybeans for soy milk. Wheat bran may be substituted.

PREHEAT OVEN TO 350°F (340°F FOR GLASS)
8 × 10 METAL PAN

1/3 cup cocoa
2 tablespoons oil or melted butter
1/2 cup soft tofu
1 teaspoon vanilla extract
1/4 cup unprocessed bran or okara
2/3 cup sugar
1/2 teaspoon baking powder
1/4 teaspoon salt
1/3 cup flour
1/2 cup chopped nuts

1. Combine the cocoa, oil or butter, tofu, and vanilla extract in a mixing bowl, and beat well. Add the bran or okara, sugar, baking powder, salt, and flour, and stir together quickly. If the mixture is too thick, add a few drops of water. Stir in the nuts.

2. Grease the baking pan, and spread in batter. Bake for no more than 20 minutes.

3. Cool in the pan on a rack, then cut into 20 squares.

CAROL CUTLER'S LOW-CALORIE FUDGE BROWNIES

Carol Cutler notes, "The calorie count on regular store-bought brownies will be only 10 to 15 points higher than this recipe. (And consider what you are buying—a lot of preservatives and artificial flavor, which we can all do without). But comparing the Fudge Brownies in this recipe with those usually made at home is another matter: 45 calories versus 150–180. Now that's a *big* difference. A large part of the disparity is accounted for by the amount of butter used. Here butter adds flavor but minimal fat. What is missing is the longer storage life of the brownies. They must be kept in an airtight container, for after two or three days they tend to dry out. However, these Fudge Brownies are very easy to make, so a pan of them can be whipped together whenever there is a craving."

PREHEAT OVEN TO 350°F
8 × 8 NONSTICK OR METAL PAN

1 ounce unsweetened chocolate (135 calories)
1 tablespoon water or coffee
4 tablespoons butter (408 calories)
2 eggs (154 calories)

3 tablespoons sugar (138 calories)
2 teaspoons vanilla (12 calories)
1 cup sifted cake flour (349 calories)
½ teaspoon baking powder
(3 calories)
½ teaspoon salt
⅓ cup walnuts chopped into coarse
bits (260 calories)

1. In a small pot over low heat melt together the chocolate, water or coffee, and butter. Meanwhile, beat together in a bowl the eggs and sugar until light and fluffy, adding the sugar a tablespoon at a time and beating thoroughly between each addition. Add the vanilla, scrape in the melted chocolate mixture, and beat well.

2. Resift the flour with the baking powder and salt, and stir into the chocolate batter. Finally, stir in the nuts.

3. Use a nonstick baking pan, or lightly grease a regular pan. Scrape the batter into the pan, and smooth with a spatula.

4. Bake for 15 minutes. Remove from the oven and cool.

5. Cut into 32 rectangles by slicing into 4 equal strips in one direction and 8 in the other. Keep the brownies in an airtight container.

·9·

CUPS AND FANCIES

❖

No matter how much everyone loves brownies in their basic square form, there is a special appeal in taking the brownie one step further. Brownie cups and fancies create new possibilities in enjoyment. No brownie lover will want to pass up the Cream Cheese-Filled Chocolate Cupcakes, in which an entire little cake of moist chocolate holds a cream cheese filling studded with miniature chocolate chips. A similar variety of tastes and textures is found in Peanut Butter-Filled Brownie Cups.

The natural affinity of brownies and ice cream is perfectly met in Brownie Ice Cream Sandwiches or Brownie Waffles with ice cream and warm chocolate sauce. With or without ice cream, brownies in cookie form will be eaten by handfuls. Who can resist Superfragilistic Drops, almost pure chocolate drops filled with chocolate chips, or Baker's German's Sweet Brownie Drops?

Still more brownie fantasies come in layers. One of my favorites, Trilevel Decadence, is a dark, fudgy semi-sweet brownie topped with a layer of buttercream and then a semi-sweet chocolate glaze. Marshmallow Cream-Topped Brownies are popular with teenagers. The cocoa brownie base is topped with marshmallow cream and drizzled with chocolate icing. Other layered

favorites are a vanilla and chocolate double-decker brownie and Mint-Topped Brownies.

For gift giving, a variety of brownie bonbons makes an interesting replacement for the more usual box of chocolates or imported crackers and cheese. You might pack an ornamental box with an assortment of brownie sandwiches, voluptuously filled with buttercream, cut into delicate fingers (see page 13) and laid in attractive rows. As a visual counterpoint to vertically stacked sandwiches, I place some on their sides to reveal a thin ribbon of contrasting frosting between two brownie layers. Even the basic brownie purist can't help but be tempted.

BAKER'S GERMAN'S SWEET BROWNIE DROPS

There's lots of mild but full-flavored chocolate in this brownielike cookie.

PREHEAT OVEN TO 350°F
LIGHTLY GREASED BAKING SHEETS

    8 *ounces Baker's German's Sweet Chocolate*
    1 *tablespoon butter*
  ¼ *cup stirred all-purpose flour*
  ¼ *teaspoon baking powder*
  ⅛ *teaspoon salt*
    2 *large eggs at room temperature*
  ¾ *cup granulated sugar*
  ½ *teaspoon vanilla extract*
  ¾ *cup finely chopped nuts*

1. In a small pan within a larger pan over simmering water or a double boiler, melt the chocolate and butter. Mix well, and let cool slightly.

2. Combine flour, baking powder, and salt, and mix well.

3. Beat eggs until foamy, and add sugar about 2 tablespoons at a time, beating 6 minutes or until eggs are the consistency of whipped cream. Stir in vanilla extract, chocolate mixture, flour mixture, and nuts.

4. Drop by teaspoonful onto greased baking sheets. Bake about 10 minutes or until cookies are just set.

5. Remove from pans and cool on racks. Makes about 3 dozen cookies.

VARIATIONS

1. Substitute ⅔ cup chopped dried cherries and ¼ cup finely chopped nuts for the ¾ cup nuts.

2. Add ½ teaspoon almond extract in addition to vanilla extract, and use almonds for the nuts.

3. Add 1½ teaspoons instant coffee powder to the flour mixture.

SUPERFRAGILISTIC DROPS

The title says it all.

PREHEAT OVEN TO 350°F
LIGHTLY GREASED COOKIE SHEETS

    1   ounce unsweetened chocolate
    7   ounces semisweet chocolate
    2   tablespoons butter
    2   large eggs

    ¼   teaspoon salt
    2   tablespoons granulated sugar
    ⅔   cup packed golden brown sugar
    ½   teaspoon vanilla extract
    ¼   teaspoon baking soda
    ¼   cup stirred all-purpose flour
 1⅔   cup chopped walnuts or pecans or
        1 cup semisweet chocolate
        morsels and 1 cup chopped
        walnuts

1. In a small pan within a larger pan over simmering water or a double boiler, melt chocolates and butter together; let cool slightly.

2. Beat eggs and salt together until thick and light in color. Add granulated sugar, and beat again until light. Beat in brown sugar until light. Beat in vanilla extract, baking soda, and cooled chocolate mixture. Stir in flour just to blend. Fold in nuts or nuts and morsels. Chill 15 minutes.

3. Drop by scant tablespoonful about 1½ inches apart onto cookie sheets.

4. Bake about 12 minutes or until top is dry and cookies are barely firm.

5. Cool cookies until they can be lifted with a pancake turner. Then remove to racks to cool completely. Makes about 60.

VARIATION

1. Add 1 teaspoon instant coffee powder with flour.

2. Add ¼ teaspoon almond extract in addition to the vanilla extract, and use 1½ cups chopped almonds.

FUDGY BROWNIE BONBONS

Baked in tiny muffin cups, these bonbons offer just a bite or two of sublime fudginess.

PREHEAT OVEN TO 450°F
2 MUFFIN PANS WITH MINIATURE CUPS
  (1 INCH IN DIAMETER)

>   1 *ounce unsweetened chocolate*
>   4 *ounces semisweet chocolate*
>   ½ *cup butter at room temperature*
>   ¼ *teaspoon salt*
>   ⅔ *cup granulated sugar*
>   2 *large eggs lightly beaten*
>   2 *tablespoons light corn syrup*
>   ½ *teaspoon vanilla extract*
>   ¼ *teaspoon almond extract*
>   ½ *cup stirred all-purpose flour*

1. In a medium pan within a larger pan over simmering water or a double boiler, melt chocolates. Mix well, and remove from heat.

2. With an electric mixer beat butter, salt, and sugar until fluffy.

3. Add eggs one at a time, beating each in very well. Beat in corn syrup, vanilla extract, and almond extract. Beat in chocolate mixture just to blend. Gently stir in flour.

4. Line muffin pans with paper cups, and fill only two-thirds full with batter. Keep any remaining batter cool until ready to bake; if it is left over after pans are filled, save for a second batch. The recipe makes about 36 bonbons.

5. Place muffin pans, evenly spaced, in oven. Immediately turn temperature down to 400°F. Bake 12–15 minutes or until a wooden toothpick inserted three-quarters of the way in from a bonbon edge comes out clean.

6. Cool in the pans on racks until bonbons can be handled. Remove from pans, and cool completely on racks to room temperature.

7. Store in a tin or tightly wrapped in foil, then a plastic bag, to avoid drying out.

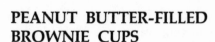
PEANUT BUTTER-FILLED BROWNIE CUPS

This is the brownie lover's version of one of America's most popular candies.

PREHEAT OVEN TO 350°F
2 CUPCAKE PANS WITH 6 CUPS
   (2 INCHES IN DIAMETER)

> 4 *ounces semisweet chocolate*
> 1 *cup butter or margarine at room*
>   *temperature*
> 1⅓ *cups granulated sugar*
> 4 *large eggs*
> 1 *teaspoon vanilla extract*
> 1¼ *cups sifted all-purpose flour*
> 3 *level tablespoons peanut butter*

1. In a small pan within a larger pan over simmering water or a double boiler, melt chocolate; let cool slightly.

2. In a food processor or with an electric mixer, cream butter or margarine and sugar together until light and fluffy. Beat in eggs and vanilla extract until mixture is smooth. Stir in flour just to mix.

3. Remove ⅓ cup of the batter to a small bowl. Add to it the 3 level tablespoons peanut butter; mix well.

4. Mix chocolate into remaining batter.

5. If you are not using paper liners, spray or lightly grease muffin tins.

6. Using two-thirds of the chocolate batter, fill muffin cups a little more than half full. Top each with a little mound of peanut butter filling. Cover with remaining chocolate batter. The peanut butter filling should be higher than the center of the cup, as it tends to sink slightly during baking. If you want to make 14 cups, use individual foil muffin cups for the two extra brownies.

7. Bake cups in the center of the oven 30–35 minutes or until a wooden toothpick inserted slightly off center comes out barely moist.

8. Cool in the pans on racks about 3 hours or until completely cool.

BIG FUDGE CUPS

PREHEAT OVEN TO 350°F
2 CUPCAKE PANS WITH 6 CUPS
   (2 INCHES IN DIAMETER)

> 8 *ounces semisweet chocolate*
> ½ *cup butter*
> ⅔ *cup granulated sugar*
> 2 *large eggs*
> ¾ *teaspoon vanilla extract*
> ¾ *cup sifted all-purpose flour*
> 1 *cup chopped nuts*

1. In a heavy medium saucepan over very low heat or in a double boiler, melt chocolate and butter together. Remove from heat, and stir until smooth and satiny.

2. Mix in sugar. Add eggs one at a time, beating each in well. Stir in vanilla extract, and then blend in flour and nuts.

3. Line cupcake pans with paper, fill two-thirds full. Bake, evenly spaced, in the center of the oven 27–35 minutes or until the tops are dry and a wooden toothpick inserted ¾ inch from the center comes out barely moist.

4. Cool in the pans on racks until cups can be handled. Remove from pans, and cool completely before wrapping in foil or plastic or placing in a tin to store.

VARIATIONS

1. EXTRA SEMISWEET FUDGY CUPS. Use 1 ounce unsweetened chocolate, 7 ounces semisweet chocolate, and ¾ cup sugar.

2. FUDGY CUPS WITH WHITE CHOCOLATE CHUNKS. Substitute ½ chopped almonds for the nuts, and add 5 ounces Tobler white chocolate. Chop each chocolate section (there are 24 in each bar) into 6 pieces, and fold in with nuts. Stir into batter.

BROWNIE CUPCAKES

Brownies in the round.

PREHEAT OVEN TO 350°F
3 CUPCAKE PANS WITH 6 CUPS
   (2 INCHES IN DIAMETER)

    4 *ounces semisweet chocolate*
    1 *cup butter or margarine*
    4 *large eggs*
 1⅓ *cups granulated sugar*
    1 *teaspoon vanilla extract*
    1 *cup sifted all-purpose flour*
    1 *cup walnut or pecan pieces*
       frosting (optional)

1. In a medium heavy saucepan over very low heat, melt chocolate and butter together. Remove from heat, blend well, and let cool to room temperature.

2. Beat eggs, sugar, and vanilla extract together until well blended. Stir in chocolate mixture. Fold in flour and nuts just until blended.

4. Line cupcake pans with paper cups, and spoon in batter. Bake 32–40 minutes or until a wooden toothpick inserted in the center comes out barely moist.

5. Cool on racks, and top, if you wish, with any chocolate frosting.

CHOCOLATE CHIP–CREAM CHEESE–FILLED BROWNIE CUPCAKES

PREHEAT OVEN TO 350°F
2 CUPCAKE PANS WITH 6 CUPS
  (2 INCHES IN DIAMETER)

> Chocolate Chip–Cream Cheese
>   Filling (below)

1½ cups sifted all-purpose flour
1 cup granulated sugar
6 tablespoons unsweetened cocoa
1 teaspoon baking soda
½ teaspoon salt
1 cup water
⅓ cup vegetable oil
1 tablespoon distilled vinegar
1 teaspoon vanilla extract
⅓ cup finely chopped nuts

1. Prepare Chocolate Chip–Cream Cheese Filling; chill until firm.

2. In a food processor or in a medium bowl of electric mixer, combine flour, sugar, cocoa, baking soda, and salt; mix well. Add water, oil, vinegar, and vanilla extract; blend again.

3. Line muffin cups with paper cups, and fill one-third full with batter. Top with a rounded teaspoonful of Chocolate Chip–Cream Cheese Filling. Top filling with remaining batter and sprinkle with nuts.

4. Bake in the center of the oven 30–35 minutes or until the top is firm.

5. Cool in the pans on racks until cupcakes can be handled. Remove from pans, and cool completely on racks.

CHOCOLATE CHIP–CREAM CHEESE FILLING

8 ounces cream cheese at room
    temperature
1 large egg
⅓ cup granulated sugar
½ teaspoon vanilla extract
¾ cup semisweet mini-morsels

1. Combine cream cheese, egg, sugar, and vanilla extract; blend well.

2. Stir in semisweet mini-morsels. Chill filling until completely firm.

CHOCOLATE-VANILLA LAYERED BROWNIES

A layer of nut-filled vanilla brownie topped with a dark chocolate brownie layer.

PREHEAT OVEN TO 350°F (340°F FOR GLASS)
9 × 9 METAL PAN

    2 ounces unsweetened chocolate
    ¾ cup butter or margarine at room
        temperature
    ¼ teaspoon salt
 1½ cups granulated sugar
    3 large eggs
 1¼ teaspoons vanilla extract
 1¼ cups stirred all-purpose flour
    ¾ cup walnut or pecan pieces

1. In a small pan within a larger pan over simmering water or a double boiler, melt chocolate; let cool to room temperature.

2. In a food processor or with an electric mixer, cream butter or margarine, salt, and sugar together until light and fluffy. Add eggs one at a time, beating each in well. Beat in vanilla extract, and stir in 1 cup of the flour by hand.

3. Remove one-third of the batter to another bowl, and stir in melted chocolate.

4. Mix remaining ¼ cup flour and the nuts into the vanilla batter.

5. Spray or lightly grease baking pan, and spread vanilla-nut batter in evenly. Spread chocolate batter over vanilla batter.

6. Bake in the center of the oven about 35 minutes or until the top is dry and a wooden toothpick inserted ½ inch from the center comes out barely moist.

7. Cool completely in the pan on a rack before cutting into 20 or 24 bars.

MINT-TOPPED BROWNIES

Chocolate-peppermint patties form a minty frosting on these fudgy brownies.

PREHEAT OVEN TO 350°F (340°F FOR GLASS)
9 × 9 METAL PAN

       3 ounces unsweetened chocolate
       6 tablespoons butter or margarine
    1⅓ cups granulated sugar
       3 large eggs
       1 teaspoon vanilla extract
    ⅔ cup sifted all-purpose flour
    ⅔ cup chopped walnuts (optional)
 16–18 chocolate-peppermint patties

1. In a heavy small pan over very low heat or in a double boiler, melt chocolate and butter or margarine together. Remove from heat, and blend well; let cool slightly.

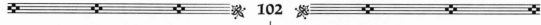
2. In a food processor, with an electric mixer, or by hand, beat sugar, eggs, and vanilla extract together. Blend in chocolate mixture. Mix in flour by hand just to mix. Mix in nuts, if you are using them.

3. Spray or lightly grease pan, and spread in batter. Bake in the center of the oven 25–35 minutes (20 minutes for glass pans) or until a wooden toothpick inserted 1 inch from the center comes out barely moist.

4. Remove brownies from oven, and arrange peppermint patties evenly over the surface. Return to oven about 3 minutes to soften patties. Remove from oven, and spread patties to cover the entire surface.

5. Cool in the pan on a rack, preferably overnight. Chill for easier cutting. With a long, thin, sharp knife cut into 30 or 36 brownies, wiping knife after each cut with a damp paper towel.

RASPBERRY TORTE BROWNIES

The divine raspberry and chocolate flavor combines in this semisweet brownie, filled with seedless raspberry preserves and iced with a chocolate-raspberry frosting.

PREHEAT OVEN TO 350°F (340°F FOR GLASS)
9 × 9 METAL PAN

      4 ounces unsweetened chocolate
     ½ cup unsalted butter cut into 5
          pieces
      3 large eggs
     ¼ teaspoon salt
   1½ teaspoons vanilla extract
   1⅓ cups granulated sugar
      1 cup sifted all-purpose flour
     ⅔ cup chopped walnuts or almonds
          (optional)
  ¼–⅓ cup seedless raspberry jam
          Raspberry-Chocolate Frosting
          (below)

1. Line pan with parchment or foil as directed on page 12.

2. In a small pan within a larger pan over simmering water or a double boiler, melt chocolate. Then add butter one piece at a time, stirring until each is incorporated into the chocolate. Remove from heat, and let cool.

3. In the medium bowl of an electric mixer, beat eggs, salt, and vanilla extract until thick and light in color. Gradually add sugar while continuing to beat eggs about 3 minutes more or until they are quite thick.

4. Thoroughly blend in chocolate mixture. Stir in flour and nuts just until blended.

5. Pour into prepared pan, and bake in the center of the oven 30–35 minutes or until a wooden toothpick inserted 1 inch from the center comes out barely moist.

6. Cool on a rack. When cool, invert brownies onto a plate, and gently peel away paper. Wrap in plastic wrap, and cover with foil. Chill before continuing.

7. While brownie is chilling, make Raspberry-Chocolate Frosting.

8. With a long, sharp, thin knife, cut brownie in half vertically. Then cut each half horizontally into two layers as follows: score cake halfway between top and bottom completely around edges. Cut through the cake, sawing back and forth, using the score marks as a guide to make two even layers.

9. Spread cut side of two layers with the raspberry jam; top with remaining layers. Spread layers with Raspberry-Chocolate Frosting. When frosting is firm, trim any rough edges. Cut each half

of the cake into 2 lengthwise strips and each strip into 8 or 9 fingers.

RASPBERRY-CHOCOLATE FROSTING

> 1½ *ounces unsweetened chocolate*
> 3 *tablespoons unsalted butter at room temperature*
> 4 *tablespoons seedless raspberry jam*
> ⅔ *cup powdered sugar*

1. In a small pan within a larger pan over simmering water or a double boiler, melt chocolate. Let cool slightly.

2. Beat butter and jam together as smoothly as possible. Gradually beat in about one-half of the sugar. Beat in cooled melted chocolate and remaining sugar. Cool slightly.

❖

SACHER TORTE BROWNIES

The treasured and traditional Viennese chocolate torte with apricot preserves and a rich chocolate glaze is transformed here into equally wonderful brownies.

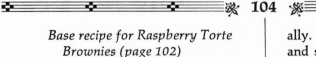
Base recipe for Raspberry Torte
   Brownies (page 102)
⅓–½ cup good-quality apricot jam
   Rich Chocolate Glaze (below)

1. Prepare brownie layers as described in Raspberry Torte Brownies.

2. Remove any large pieces of apricot from the preserves, and mince finely. Stir back into preserves. Fill brownies, substituting about ⅓–½ cup apricot preserves for the raspberry jam.

3. Make the Rich Chocolate Glaze, and let cool almost to room temperature. Spoon over brownies. Let glaze set completely.

4. Cut each filled brownie half into 3 long, thin strips. Lay each strip on its side with the glaze facing you, and cut into 4 or 5 fingers.

RICH CHOCOLATE GLAZE

3 ounces semisweet chocolate
2 tablespoons butter
2 teaspoons Cointreau, cognac, or
   brandy

1. In a heavy small saucepan, melt chocolate and butter, stirring occasion-ally. When melted, remove from heat, and stir until smooth and satiny.

2. Blend in Cointreau, cognac, or brandy.

❖

TRILEVEL DECADENCE

A very dark semisweet brownie topped with a layer of buttercream and glazed with dark chocolate.

PREHEAT OVEN TO 350°F (340°F FOR GLASS)
9 × 9 METAL PAN

3 ounces unsweetened chocolate
½ cup unsalted butter at room
   temperature
1 cup granulated sugar
3 large eggs
¼ teaspoon salt
1¼ teaspoons vanilla extract
½ cup stirred all-purpose flour
1 cup chopped walnuts
¾ cup Pâtissière Buttercream
   (page 154) or French Custard
   Buttercream (page 152)
   Extra-Dark Chocolate Glaze
   (below)

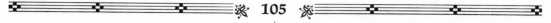
1. In a small pan within a larger pan over simmering water or a double boiler, melt the chocolate. Let cool to room temperature.

2. In a food processor or with an electric mixer, cream butter until fluffy. Add sugar in thirds, continuing to beat until mixture is light and creamy. Add eggs one at a time, beating each in well. Beat in salt, vanilla extract, and melted chocolate. Stir in flour and nuts by hand just until incorporated.

3. Lightly grease pan or line with paper (page 12), and spread in batter. Bake in the center of the oven 18–22 minutes or until the top is dry and a wooden toothpick inserted ½ inch from the center comes out barely moist.

4. Cool in the pan on a rack. Invert onto a plate, and gently peel away paper. Invert a second time. Chill brownie before continuing.

5. While brownie is cooling, make buttercream. Spread evenly over brownie. Chill until firm.

6. Make glaze. When it is cool, smooth evenly over buttercream, and spread with a knife. Allow to set.

7. Protect set glaze with a film of plastic wrap before wrapping brownie in foil to store.

8. Before serving, trim brownie edges with a long, sharp, thin knife. Cut brownie into 5 strips, wiping knife blade with a damp towel after each cut. Turn each strip on its side, with the glaze facing you, and cut into 4 or 5 bars. This keeps both frosting and glaze intact.

EXTRA-DARK CHOCOLATE GLAZE

3 ounce bar Lindt or Tobler
extra-bittersweet chocolate
broken into pieces
3 tablespoons boiling water
¼ teaspoon instant espresso powder
1 tablespoon brandy or cognac

1. Combine all ingredients in a heavy small pan, and cook over very low heat, stirring constantly until chocolate melts.

2. Remove from heat, stir to blend thoroughly, and let cool to room temperature but not firm before spooning over brownie.

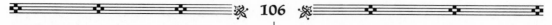
MARSHMALLOW CREAM–TOPPED BROWNIES

Cocoa brownies topped with a marshmallow cream frosting and glazed with Butter-Cocoa Topping. This recipe is ours compliments of Mrs. John Burkley of Kansas City, Missouri.

PREHEAT OVEN TO 325°F
9 × 13 METAL PAN

>   1   cup butter at room temperature
>   2   cups granulated sugar
>   ⅓   cup unsweetened cocoa
>   4   large eggs
> 1½   teaspoons vanilla extract
> 1¼   cups sifted all-purpose flour
>   1   cup chopped pecans
>   7-ounce jar marshmallow cream
>   Butter-Cocoa Topping (below)

1. In a food processor or with an electric mixer, cream butter and 1 cup of the sugar until light and fluffy. Beat in cocoa and remaining sugar until mixture is fluffy. Add eggs, one at a time, beating each in well. Beat in vanilla extract. Stir in flour just to blend. Stir in pecans.

2. Lightly grease or spray pan, and spread in batter. Bake in the center of the oven about 25 minutes or until a wooden toothpick inserted 1 inch from the center comes out barely moist.

3. Cool brownies in the pan on a rack.

4. When brownies are cool, warm marshmallow cream in a double boiler or in a pan in a larger pan of hot water. Spread over brownies, and chill.

5. While brownies are chilling, prepare Butter-Cocoa Topping. With a warm spatula, smooth topping over marshmallow cream. Chill before cutting into 32 brownies.

BUTTER-COCOA TOPPING

>   ¼   cup unsalted butter at room
>   temperature
>   3   tablespoons unsweetened cocoa
>   3   cups powdered sugar
>   1   teaspoon vanilla extract
> 2–3   tablespoons milk

1. Beat together butter and cocoa. Gradually beat in powdered sugar and then vanilla extract.

2. Add just enough milk to make frosting spreadable.

BROWNIE ICE CREAM SANDWICHES

This brownie tastes good cold.

PREHEAT OVEN TO 350°F (340°F FOR GLASS)
2 9 × 9 METAL PANS

5 *ounces unsweetened chocolate*
⅓ *cup butter at room temperature*
⅓ *cup vegetable shortening at room temperature*
1½ *cups granulated sugar*
4 *large eggs*
¼ *teaspoon salt*
¼ *teaspoon almond extract (optional)*
2 *teaspoons vanilla extract*
1 *cup sifted all-purpose flour*
1½ *cups chopped walnuts*
1 *pint ice cream (flavor of your choice)*
lightly sweetened whipped cream or chocolate sauce (optional)

1. In a small pan within a larger pan over simmering water or in a double boiler, melt the chocolate. Let cool to room temperature.

2. In a food processor or with an electric mixer, cream butter and shortening together until fluffy. Add sugar in thirds, continuing to beat until mixture is light and creamy. Add eggs one at a time, beating each in well. Beat in salt, almond and vanilla extracts, and melted chocolate. Fold in flour and nuts by hand just until incorporated.

3. Lightly grease or paper-line pans (page 12), and pour in batter. Bake in the center of the oven 18–25 minutes or until the tops are dry and a wooden toothpick inserted ½ inch from the center comes out barely moist.

4. Cool in the pans on rack. Invert onto plates, and gently peel away paper. Invert a second time. Chill brownie before continuing.

5. Spread ice cream evenly over one brownie layer, and top with the other layer. Press gently and firmly to even out filling. Remove excess filling from sides of brownie. Wrap in plastic wrap, and chill until set.

6. To serve, trim away any ragged edges with a long, sharp, thin knife. Cut sandwich into 4 long strips. Turn strips on their sides, and cut each strip into 3 or 4 bars.

7. Serve brownies on a plate to be eaten with a knife and fork. Garnish with whipped cream or chocolate sauce if you wish.

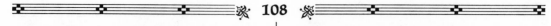
BROWNIE SANDWICHES

1. Make layers for brownie sandwiches using the recipe for either Grasshopper Brownies (page 45) or Brownie Ice Cream Sandwiches (page 107).

2. Fill and cut brownies as directed in Grasshopper Brownies.

Here is a list of complementary frostings and fillings:

FOR THE GRASSHOPPER BROWNIE LAYERS

Coffee-Brandy Buttercream (page 35)
Semisweet Chocolate Icing (page 156)
Dark Chocolate Frosting (page 155)
French Custard Buttercream (page 152)
Raspberry-Chocolate Frosting
    (page 103)

FOR ICE CREAM SANDWICH BROWNIE LAYERS

Whiskey Cream (page 48)
Pâtissière Buttercream (page 154)
Quick Vanilla Buttercream (page 153)
Orange Buttercream (page 33)

BROWNIE WAFFLES

Brownie waffles are not necessarily breakfast fare. They make a fine dessert dusted with powdered sugar or served as a base for an ice cream sundae. Brownie waffle ice cream sandwiches, garnished with whipped cream, are another festive dessert.

PREHEAT A WAFFLE BAKER WHILE
    PREPARING BATTER

> 1½ cups (9 ounces) semisweet
>   chocolate morsels
> ¾ cup milk
> ½ cup butter or margarine
> 1½ cups sifted cake flour
> ½ teaspoon baking powder
> ½ teaspoon salt
> 2 large eggs separated and left to
>   stand until room temperature
> 6 tablespoons granulated sugar
> ½ cup finely chopped walnuts
>   powdered sugar or garnishes

1. In a heavy small saucepan combine chocolate morsels, milk, and butter. Cook over very low heat, stirring occasionally, until chocolate and butter have melted. Remove from heat, and stir until mixture is completely smooth and well blended.

2. Combine flour, baking powder and salt. Mix well.

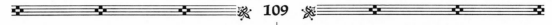
3. In the medium bowl of an electric mixer, beat egg yolks until thick and light in color. Gradually beat in sugar. Beat in chocolate mixture until smooth. Stir in flour mixture and nuts only until blended.

4. In a clean bowl with clean beaters, beat egg whites until curved peaks will hold their shape when beaters are gently lifted. Fold half of the whites into the chocolate batter, then fold in remaining whites.

5. Spoon batter into the center of the waffle baker, allowing about 3 tablespoons for each section. Lower cover, and bake 7–8 minutes or until steaming stops. Do not raise cover during baking period. When waffle is baked, lift cover, and loosen waffle with fork, carefully removing one section at a time.

6. Serve warm or cooled with suggested embellishments.

Makes 6 servings.

·10·

BIG-PAN BROWNIES

❖

These big-pan recipes are designed for bake sales, large gatherings, or someone who likes to keep a plentiful supply of brownies on hand. And here is a hint on cutting large pans of brownies from Maida Heatter. With a ruler, mark sections of brownie with toothpick "markers" to help you cut straight lines. Once brownies have been cut the long way, mark horizontal slices with toothpicks, and cut once again.

It's also nice to wrap brownies individually in plastic wrap or varied colors of florist's foil for gift giving or to boost sales appeal.

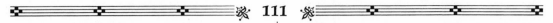
BAKE SALE BROWNIES

PREHEAT OVEN TO 350°F
15½ × 10½ × 1 JELLYROLL PAN

6 *ounces unsweetened chocolate*
1 *cup butter at room temperature*
¼ *teaspoon salt*
1¾ *cups granulated sugar*
1 *cup light brown sugar*
⅔ *cup dark corn syrup*
6 *large eggs*
2 *cups sifted all-purpose flour*
2 *cups pecan halves or coarsely
broken walnuts*

1. If you wish, line pan with foil or parchment (page 12). If not, spray or lightly grease pan.
2. In a small pan within a larger pan over simmering water or a double boiler, melt chocolate; let cool slightly.
3. In a large mixing bowl, cream butter, salt, and sugars together until light and fluffy. Beat in corn syrup and eggs one at a time until well blended. Beat in melted chocolate. Add flour, and stir until smooth. Add pecans or walnuts, and stir until evenly distributed.
4. Spread batter in prepared pan. With a small metal spatula, smooth evenly. Bake in the center of the oven about 40 minutes or until a wooden toothpick inserted in the center comes out barely moist.
5. Cool completely in the pan on a rack. Chill.
6. Invert on a large board, and if you have lined pan, remove paper. Invert brownie again. Cut into bars, making 6 evenly spaced cuts on the 15-inch side and 5 on the 10½-inch side. Wrap each brownie in plastic wrap. Store refrigerated in a container.

VARIATIONS

1. Reserve ½ cup pecans or walnuts to sprinkle over the surface of the batter before baking.
2. Add 2 teaspoons vanilla extract along with corn syrup.
3. Top with any frosting of your choice, and sprinkle with a spray of finely chopped nuts.
4. Decorate individual brownies with flowers made of sliced almonds.

BIG-PAN MARBLED BROWNIE BARS

PREHEAT OVEN TO 350°F
15½ × 10½ × 1 JELLYROLL PAN

4 ounces melted chocolate
2 cups sifted all-purpose flour
¾ teaspoon baking powder
½ teaspoon salt
1 cup plus 2 tablespoons butter
  or margarine at room
  temperature
2 cups granulated sugar
4 large eggs
1½ teaspoons vanilla extract
½ teaspoon almond extract
  (optional)
1⅓ cup chopped walnuts or almonds
  (optional)

1. In a small pan within a larger pan over simmering water or a double boiler, melt chocolate. Let cool slightly.

2. Combine flour, baking powder, and salt; blend well.

3. In the large bowl of an electric mixer, cream butter and 1 cup of the sugar until fluffy. Beat in remaining sugar and eggs, one at a time, beating each in well. Beat in vanilla extract. Beat in almond extract if you are using it.

4. Fold in flour mixture by hand. Fold in nuts if you are using them.

5. Divide batter in half. Stir melted chocolate into one half, mixing well.

6. Lightly grease or spray pan. Drop batters in mounds alternately in checkerboard fashion onto pan. Swirl batters together with a small spatula or table knife to marbleize.

7. Bake in the center of the oven 27–32 minutes or until a wooden toothpick inserted 2½ inches from the pan edge comes out clean.

8. Cool completely in the pan on a rack before cutting into 30 brownies.

BIG-PAN FUDGY BROWNIES

PREHEAT OVEN TO 350°F
15½ × 10½ × 1 JELLYROLL PAN

5½ ounces unsweetened chocolate
1⅓ cups butter or margarine
2½ cups granulated sugar
¼ teaspoon salt
1½ teaspoons vanilla extract
5 large eggs
1½ cups sifted all-purpose flour
1½ cups chopped walnuts or pecans

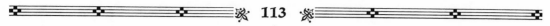
1. In a medium saucepan over very low heat or in a double boiler, melt chocolate and butter together. Let cool slightly.

2. Stir in the sugar, salt, and vanilla extract. Mix in eggs one at a time, blending each in well. Stir in flour and then nuts just to blend.

3. Lightly grease pan or line it with foil (page 12), and spread batter into it.

4. Bake in the center of the oven 25–30 minutes or until a wooden toothpick inserted 1 inch from the center comes out barely moist.

5. Cool completely in the pan on a rack before cutting into 35 brownies.

❖

BIG-PAN MARSHMALLOW-TOPPED BROWNIES

PREHEAT OVEN TO 350°F
15½ × 10½ × 1 JELLYROLL PAN

1 cup butter or margarine
6 tablespoons unsweetened cocoa
4 large eggs
¼ teaspoon salt

1 teaspoon vanilla extract
1¾ cups granulated sugar
1½ cups sifted all-purpose flour
1½ cups chopped walnuts or pecans
3 cups miniature marshmallows
Chocolate Glaze 3 (below)

1. In a medium saucepan melt butter. Remove from heat, and stir in cocoa. Return to heat, and stir until mixture is smooth.

2. In the large bowl of an electric mixer, combine eggs, salt, vanilla extract, and sugar; beat until well blended. Add flour alternately with butter mixture, blending well. Fold in nuts.

3. Lightly grease or spray pan, and spread in batter.

4. Bake in the center of the oven 18–20 minutes or until a wooden toothpick inserted 2 inches from the pan edge comes out clean. Remove from the oven, and sprinkle evenly with marshmallows. Return to the oven 2 minutes, and then remove again and press marshmallows lightly to flatten slightly.

5. Cool in the pan on a rack to slightly above room temperature. While brownie is still warm, pour on glaze.

6. Cool completely before cutting into 35 brownies.

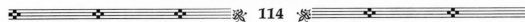
CHOCOLATE GLAZE 3

2½ ounces unsweetened chocolate
¼ cup butter
⅛ teaspoon salt
3 tablespoons hot water
1¾ cups powdered sugar
1 teaspoon vanilla extract

1. In a small pan over very low heat or in a double boiler, melt chocolate and butter together; let cool slightly.

2. Stir in water, powdered sugar, and vanilla extract, and beat with a spoon until mixture is smooth and thick.

BIG-PAN PEANUT BUTTER BROWNIES

PREHEAT OVEN TO 350°F
15½ × 10½ × 1 JELLYROLL PAN

2¼ cups stirred all-purpose flour
2 teaspoons baking powder
½ teaspoon salt
⅓ cup creamy peanut butter
½ cup butter or margarine at room
      temperature
1 cup granulated sugar
1½ cups packed light brown sugar
3 large eggs at room temperature
1½ teaspoons vanilla extract
¾ cup chopped roasted, unsalted
      peanuts or 1½ cups semisweet
      or milk chocolate morsels

1. Combine flour, baking powder, and salt; mix well.

2. In the large bowl of an electric mixer, cream peanut butter, butter, and granulated sugar together until smooth and creamy. Beat in brown sugar. Add eggs one at a time, beating each in well. Beat in vanilla extract.

3. Fold in flour mixture in thirds, just to mix. Fold in either nuts or chocolate morsels.

4. Lightly grease or spray pan, and spread in batter. Carefully even out batter with a spatula.

5. Bake in the center of the oven about 25 minutes or until a wooden toothpick inserted 1½ inches from the center comes out barely moist.

6. Cool completely in the pan on a rack before cutting into 35 brownies.

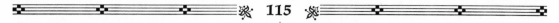
BIG-PAN BLONDIES

PREHEAT OVEN TO 350°F
15½ × 10½ × 1 JELLYROLL PAN

> 2½ cups stirred all-purpose flour
> 2 teaspoons baking powder
> ½ teaspoon salt
> ¾ cup butter at room temperature
> ¾ cup granulated sugar
> 1¼ cups packed golden brown sugar
> 1½ teaspoons vanilla extract
> 3 large eggs at room temperature
> 1½ cups chopped walnuts or pecans

1. Combine flour, baking powder, and salt; mix well.

2. In the large bowl of an electric mixer, combine butter and granulated sugar; beat until light in color. Add brown sugar, and beat until smooth. Add vanilla extract and eggs one at a time, beating each in well.

3. Add flour mixture in thirds, mixing just until blended. Blend in nuts.

4. Lightly grease or spray pan, and spread in batter.

5. Bake in the center of the oven 25–30 minutes or until a wooden toothpick inserted 1 inch from center comes out clean.

6. Cut into 30 or 36 blondies.

VARIATION

1. Stir in 2½ teaspoons ground cinnamon with the flour.

·11·

BEYOND THE BASICS

OTHER CHOCOLATE BROWNIES

After grouping brownies into distinct categories—deluxe, nut, fruit, unchocolate, healthful, cups and fancies, and desserts—there still remain many tantalizing variations on the brownie theme. Starting with Chocolate Cheesecake Brownies and their relatives, Layered Cream Cheese, Marbled Cream Cheese Swirl, and Raspberry Cream Cheese Swirl, we progress to the Three-Textured Chocolate, with its thin, crisp layer of chocolate oatmeal cookie topped with a moist brownie filling and a chocolate glaze. The chocolate swirl brownie, a light chocolate base swirled with a semisweet chocolate ganache, is another interesting entry in this collection, as are the Chocolate Chip Oatmeal Brownies, made without flour.

Here, too, are the double-impact chocolate brownies—such triumphs of chocolate combination as Milk Chocolate Brownies with Extra-Dark Chocolate Glaze or Semisweet Brownies with Milk Chocolate Chips or Double Chocolate Brownies, a fudge brownie with chocolate chips.

A well-known chef is also represented in this section. Abby Mandel's Toffee Fudge Brownies are unforgettable. And in this chapter you'll find such favorites

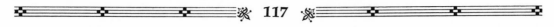
as Chocolate Marshmallow, Rocky Road Brownies, No-Bake Brownies, Spicy Fudge Brownies, and more. All that remains is for you to be inspired to create a chocolate variety of your own.

MILK CHOCOLATE BROWNIES WITH EXTRA-DARK CHOCOLATE GLAZE

I used Ghirardelli milk chocolate to test this recipe. I thought it made a perfectly balanced flavor combination with the extra bittersweet chocolate glaze.

PREHEAT OVEN TO 350°F (340°F FOR GLASS)
9 × 9 METAL PAN

9	*ounces milk chocolate*
2½	*tablespoons butter*
¾	*cup stirred all-purpose flour*
¼	*teaspoon salt*
½	*teaspoon baking powder*
3	*large eggs*
½	*teaspoon vanilla extract*
6	*tablespoons granulated sugar*
1	*cup chopped walnuts*
	Extra-Dark Chocolate Glaze
	(page 105)

1. In a small pan within a larger pan over simmering water or a double boiler, melt chocolate and butter together. Remove from heat, and stir until smooth and satiny.

2. Combine flour, salt, and baking powder; blend well.

3. In a food processor or with an electric mixer, beat eggs, vanilla extract, and sugar together until light in color. Stir in chocolate mixture. Stir in flour and nuts just to blend.

4. Spray or lightly grease pan, and spread in batter. Bake in the center of the oven 30–35 minutes or until a wooden toothpick inserted 1 inch from the center comes out barely moist.

5. Cool completely in the pan on a rack. When cool, glaze with Extra-Dark Chocolate Glaze, and chill. While chilled, cut into 25 brownies. Serve at room temperature.

CHOCOLATE CHIP VARIATION

1. Omit chocolate glaze. Reduce nuts to ⅔ cup, and stir ¾ cup semisweet chocolate morsels into the batter when adding nuts.

THREE-TEXTURED CHOCOLATE

Absolute dynamite for chocolate lovers. A thin layer of chocolate oatmeal cookie crust topped with a moist fudgy brownie and glazed with semisweet chocolate—divine.

PREHEAT OVEN TO 350°F (340°F FOR GLASS)
9 × 9 METAL PAN

      2 *ounces semisweet chocolate*
      7 *tablespoons butter*
     ½ *cup sifted all-purpose flour*
      1 *cup quick-cooking oats*
     ⅛ *teaspoon baking soda*
     ½ *cup packed golden brown sugar*
      3 *ounces unsweetened chocolate*
     ⅔ *cup stirred all-purpose flour*
     ¼ *teaspoon salt*
     ¼ *teaspoon baking powder*

     ½ *cup unsalted butter at room*
          temperature
      1 *cup granulated sugar*
      3 *large eggs*
   1¼ *teaspoons vanilla extract*
     ⅔ *cup walnut pieces*
     ½ *cup semisweet chocolate morsels*

1. In a small pan within a larger pan over simmering water or a double boiler, melt semisweet chocolate and 6 tablespoons butter. Mix well until smooth and satiny.

2. Combine the ½ cup sifted flour, oats, baking soda, and brown sugar; mix well.

3. Pour melted chocolate mixture over oat mixture, and mix thoroughly. Spray or lightly grease pan, and pat in mixture. Bake in the center of the oven 12 minutes. Cool about 20 minutes on a rack.

4. Meanwhile, melt unsweetened chocolate as directed in step 1.

5. Combine the ⅔ cup stirred flour, salt, and baking powder.

6. Cream the ½ cup unsalted butter until fluffy with an electric mixer. Gradually add sugar, beating until light and creamy. Add eggs one at a time, beating each in well. On low speed mix in vanilla extract and unsweetened chocolate. Stir in flour mixture and nuts by hand.

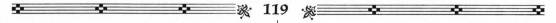
7. Pour batter over the cooled oat base, and bake in the center of the oven 30–35 minutes or until a wooden toothpick inserted ½ inch from the center comes out barely moist.

8. Cool cake in the pan on a rack 6 hours or overnight.

9. Melt semisweet morsels and the remaining tablespoonful of butter together in a small heavy pan over very low heat. With a small spatula or butter knife, spread chocolate in a thin, even layer over the top of brownie. Cool or chill until firm before cutting into 30 or 36 brownies.

SEMISWEET BROWNIES WITH MILK CHOCOLATE CHIPS

PREHEAT OVEN TO 350°F (340°F FOR GLASS)
8 × 8 METAL PAN

  6 *tablespoons butter*
  6 *ounces semisweet chocolate*
  ¾ *cup stirred all-purpose flour*
  ¼ *teaspoon baking soda*
  ¼ *teaspoon salt*
  2 *large eggs*
  ⅔ *cup granulated sugar*

  1 *teaspoon vanilla extract*
  1 *cup chilled milk chocolate chips*
  ⅔ *cup chopped nuts (optional)*

1. In a heavy saucepan over very low heat or in a double boiler, melt butter and chocolate together. Mix well, remove from heat, and let cool slightly.

2. Combine flour, baking soda, and salt; mix well.

3. Beat eggs until thick and light in color. Gradually add sugar, beating until thick. Stir in vanilla extract and chocolate mixture. Fold in flour mixture, chilled chips, and nuts, if you are using them.

4. Spray or lightly grease pan, and spread in batter. Bake in the center of the oven about 35 minutes or until a wooden toothpick inserted 1 inch from the center comes out barely moist.

5. Cool completely in the pan on a rack. Chill slightly before cutting into 20 or 25 brownies.

SEMISWEET BROWNIES WITH WHITE CHOCOLATE CHUNKS

1. Follow preceding recipe, substituting 5 ounces of chilled Tobler white chocolate for the chocolate chips. Cut each section or rectangle of a white chocolate bar into 5 or 6 pieces.

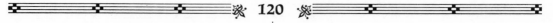
2. Chill chocolate again (the freezer is fast) before stirring into brownie batter. Omit nuts.

SOUR CREAM–BROWN SUGAR BROWNIES

A special cakelike brownie, the perfect foil for Sour Cream Chocolate Frosting (page 155) or Dark Chocolate Frosting (page 155).

PREHEAT OVEN TO 350°F (340°F FOR GLASS)
9 × 9 METAL PAN

> 2 *ounces unsweetened chocolate*
> 1 *cup sifted all-purpose flour*
> ¼ *teaspoon salt*
> ¾ *teaspoon ground cinnamon*
> ½ *teaspoon baking soda*
> ⅔ *cup butter or margarine at room temperature*
> 1 *cup packed light brown sugar*
> 1 *large egg*
> 1 *teaspoon vanilla extract*
> ⅓ *cup sour cream or yogurt*
> 1 *cup walnut or pecan pieces (optional)*
> *frosting (optional)*

1. In a small pan within a larger pan over simmering water or a double boiler, melt chocolate. Remove from heat, and cool to room temperature.

2. Combine flour, salt, cinnamon, and baking soda; mix thoroughly.

3. In a food processor or with an electric mixer, cream the butter until fluffy. Add the sugar in thirds, continuing to cream until fluffy and ivory colored.

4. Add the egg, and beat until smooth. Stir in vanilla extract, sour cream, and melted chocolate; mix well. Fold in flour mixture. Stir in nuts if you are using them, reserving a few for the topping.

5. Spray or lightly grease pan, and spread batter in it, smoothing the top.

6. Bake in the center of the oven 25–32 minutes or until the top is dry and a wooden toothpick inserted one inch from the center comes out barely moist.

7. Cool completely on a rack. When cool, frost if desired, sprinkle with a few nuts, and cut into 24 brownies.

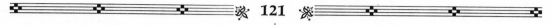
MARBLED CREAM CHEESE BROWNIES

A cream cheese filling swirls throughout a fudge brownie.

PREHEAT OVEN TO 325°F
9 × 9 METAL PAN

    Swirled Cream Cheese Filling
       (below)
  3 ounces unsweetened chocolate
  ⅔ cup butter or margarine
  1 cup plus 2 tablespoons stirred
     all-purpose flour
  ½ teaspoon baking powder
  ¼ teaspoon salt
  ½ cup chopped walnuts (optional)
  3 large eggs
1⅓ cups granulated sugar
  1 teaspoon vanilla extract

1. Prepare Swirled Cream Cheese Filling.

2. In a heavy small pan over very low heat or in a double boiler, melt chocolate and butter or margarine together. Let cool to room temperature.

3. Combine flour, baking powder, and salt; and mix well. Add walnuts, if you are using them.

4. In a food processor or with an electric mixer, beat eggs until thick and light in color. Gradually beat in sugar and then vanilla extract until mixture is thick and light. Mix in chocolate mixture and then dry ingredients.

5. Lightly grease or spray pan, and spread in slightly more than half of the chocolate batter. Spoon filling evenly over the batter, and drop the remaining batter over the filling, spreading until even. Marbleize by cutting through batter with a table knife from side to side in a wide zigzag pattern.

6. Bake in the center of the oven 40–45 minutes (35–40 minutes for glass pan) or until a wooden toothpick inserted 1 inch from the center comes out barely moist.

7. Cool in the pan on a rack 6–8 hours before cutting into 30 brownies.

SWIRLED CREAM CHEESE FILLING

  2 3-ounce packages cream cheese
     at room temperature
  ⅓ cup granulated sugar
  1 tablespoon all-purpose flour
  1 large egg
  1 teaspoon vanilla extract
  ½ teaspoon lemon juice

1. In a food processor or with an electric mixer, beat all ingredients together just until smooth.

CHOCOLATE CHEESECAKE BROWNIES

This rich, dark chocolate brownie is topped with a cheesecake layer. You may want to add the Graham Cracker–Nut Crust, too. Use 11 ounces of bulk cream cheese or one 8- and one 3-ounce package for this recipe.

PREHEAT OVEN TO 350°F (340°F FOR GLASS)
9 × 9 METAL PAN

> *Graham Cracker–Nut Crust*
> *(optional; below)*
> *Cream Cheese Topping (below)*
> 6 *ounces semisweet chocolate*
> 2 *ounces cream cheese at room*
>   *temperature*
> 3 *tablespoons butter at room*
>   *temperature*
> ⅔ *cup granulated sugar*
> 2 *large eggs*
> 1 *teaspoon vanilla extract*
> ¼ *teaspoon almond extract*
>   *(optional)*
> ¼ *teaspoon salt*
> ½ *cup sifted all-purpose flour*

1. Prepare Graham Cracker–Nut Crust, if you are using it.
2. Prepare Cream Cheese Topping.
3. In a small pan within a larger pan over simmering water or a double boiler, melt chocolate; let cool slightly.
4. In a food processor or with an electric mixer, beat cheese and butter together until smooth. Beat in sugar until well incorporated. Add eggs one at a time, beating each in well. Beat in vanilla and almond extract and salt. Mix in melted chocolate. Stir in flour just to mix.
5. Pour batter into prepared crust if you are using it. If you are not using crust, lightly grease or spray pan, and spread in batter. Evenly dribble Cream Cheese Topping over the surface, smoothing it with a knife.
6. Bake in the center of the oven 50–55 minutes or until the top is dry and a circle no larger than 1½ inches in diameter remains soft in the center. A wooden toothpick inserted 2 inches from the pan edge should come out with slightly cakelike crumbs. The edges of the cake will begin to pull away very slightly from the pan. Cool to room temperature in the pan on a rack.
7. Refrigerate 8 hours or overnight. With a long, thin, sharp knife, cut into 30 or 36 small brownies, wiping knife blade with a damp cloth after each cut.

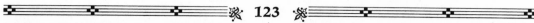
GRAHAM CRACKER–NUT CRUST

⅔ cup graham cracker crumbs
*⅓ cup very finely chopped walnuts,
    almonds, or pecans*
3 tablespoons granulated sugar
4 tablespoons melted butter

1. Combine graham cracker crumbs, chopped nuts, sugar, and melted butter.
2. Pat into the bottom of the pan, and bake in the oven 8 minutes. Cool on a rack.

CREAM CHEESE TOPPING

*9 ounces cream cheese at room
    temperature*
*2 tablespoons unsalted butter at
    room temperature*
½ teaspoon vanilla extract
⅔ cup granulated sugar
2 large eggs
3 tablespoons half and half or milk
1 tablespoon all-purpose flour

1. Beat cream cheese and butter together just until smooth.
2. Add vanilla, half of the sugar, and all the eggs; beat until incorporated.
3. Add the remaining sugar, half and half or milk, and flour; beat just until smooth.

LAYERED CREAM CHEESE BROWNIES

A cream cheese layer is swirled between two fudgy layers.

PREHEAT OVEN TO 350°F (340°F FOR GLASS)
8 × 8 METAL PAN

Cream Cheese Filling (below)
2½ ounces unsweetened chocolate
½ cup butter or margarine
¾ cup stirred all-purpose flour
½ teaspoon baking powder
½ teaspoon salt
2 large eggs
1 teaspoon vanilla extract
1 cup granulated sugar

1. Prepare Cream Cheese Filling.
2. In a heavy small pan over very low heat or a double boiler, melt chocolate and butter or margarine together. Mix thoroughly, and let cool to room temperature.
3. Combine flour, baking powder, and salt; mix well.
4. Beat eggs and vanilla extract until well mixed. Add sugar, and beat until well blended. Blend in cooled chocolate mixture. Stir in flour mixture.
5. Spray or lightly grease pan, and pour in slightly more than half of the

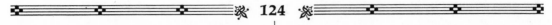
chocolate batter. Spoon Cream Cheese Filling evenly over chocolate batter, and top it with remaining batter.

6. Carefully place in the center of the oven, trying not to disturb layers when pan is moved. Bake about 35–40 minutes or until a wooden toothpick inserted ½ inch from the center comes out barely moist.

7. Cool completely in pan on a rack before cutting into 20 brownies.

CREAM CHEESE FILLING

   1 *8-ounce package cream cheese at room temperature*
  ⅓ *cup granulated sugar*
  ½ *teaspoon vanilla extract*
  1 *large egg*
  4 *teaspoons all-purpose flour*

1. In a food processor or with an electric mixer, blend all ingredients just until smooth and creamy.

NO-BAKE BROWNIES

These are a cross between fudge and brownies. They can be mixed up in minutes—and that even includes the frosting. However, they do need to chill 24 hours before being served.

9 × 9 PAN

  4 *cups graham cracker crumbs*
  1 *cup broken walnut pieces*
  ½ *cup sifted powdered sugar*
  2 *cups (12-ounce package) semisweet chocolate morsels*
  1 *cup evaporated milk*
  1 *teaspoon vanilla extract*

1. Combine crumbs, nuts, and sugar in a large bowl.

2. Melt chocolate in evaporated milk over low heat, stirring constantly. Blend into a smooth mixture. Stir in vanilla extract.

3. Remove ½ cup of the chocolate mixture from the pan. Mix remainder with the crumb-nut mixture.

4. Butter a pan well and spread in batter. Smooth the top. Spread the remaining ½ cup of chocolate mixture over the top.

5. Chill brownies 24 hours. With a long, thin, sharp knife, cut into 36 1½-inch squares, wiping knife blade with a damp towel after each cut.

NO-BAKE MOCHA BROWNIES

9 × 9 PAN

4 cups vanilla wafer crumbs
1 cup chopped walnuts or almonds
4 teaspoons instant coffee powder
8 ounces semisweet chocolate
1 cup evaporated milk
1 teaspoon vanilla extract
¼ teaspoon almond extract
(optional)

1. Combine crumbs, nuts, and coffee powder in a large mixing bowl.
2. Melt chocolate in ¾ cup of the evaporated milk over very low heat, stirring constantly. Remove from heat, and blend in vanilla and almond extracts. Remove ½ cup of the chocolate mixture, and reserve.
3. Add larger portion of the chocolate mixture and remaining ¼ cup milk to crumb mixture. Blend well.
4. Butter a pan well, and spread in crumb mixture. Spread the rest of the chocolate mixture over the top.
5. Chill 24 hours. With a long, thin, sharp knife, cut into 36 1½-inch squares, wiping knife with a damp towel after each cut.

GERMAN CHOCOLATE CAKE BROWNIES

Sumptuously filled with caramel and brimming with nuts and coconut, these brownies get raves from the most discriminating palates, although the base is a cake mix.

PREHEAT OVEN TO 350°F (340°F FOR GLASS)
9 × 13 METAL PAN

1 14-ounce bag caramels
⅔ cup evaporated milk
1 18½-ounce box Swiss chocolate cake mix
¾ cup butter, melted
1 cup semisweet chocolate morsels
½ cup flaked coconut
¾ cup chopped walnuts

1. In a small pan within a larger pan over simmering water or a double boiler, combine caramels and ⅓ cup of the evaporated milk. Stir occasionally until melted; keep warm.
2. Combine cake mix, remaining evaporated milk, and butter in the large bowl of electric mixer. Beat at medium speed 2 minutes, scraping bowl occasionally. Batter will be thick.
3. Spray or lightly grease a pan, and spread in half of the cake batter. Bake 6

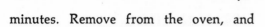
minutes. Remove from the oven, and cool on a rack 2 minutes.

4. Spread warm caramel mixture carefully over baked layer. Sprinkle with chocolate pieces and coconut.

5. Stir half of the nuts into remaining cake batter. Drop batter in small mounds over chocolate-coconut layer. Sprinkle with the remaining nuts.

6. Bake in the center of the oven 16–18 minutes or until the top springs back when lightly touched.

7. Cool completely in the pan on a rack before cutting into 36 brownies.

❖

CHOCOLATE MARSHMALLOW BROWNIES

Unlike the Rocky-Road Brownies on page 131, these brownies have marshmallows in the batter rather than on the surface. They have an interesting fudgy texture and are very chocolaty and not too sweet. If you like, a rocky-road effect may be created by sprinkling a handful of the mini-marshmallows over the surface of the brownie the last minute of baking time.

PREHEAT OVEN TO 350°F (340°F FOR GLASS)
9 × 9 METAL PAN

1½ cups mini-marshmallows
1 cup (6-ounce package) semisweet chocolate morsels
½ cup butter or margarine
2 large eggs
1 teaspoon vanilla extract
⅛ teaspoon salt
¼ teaspoon baking powder
½ cup stirred all-purpose flour
⅔ cup chopped walnuts or almonds additional mini-marshmallows (optional)

1. Combine the marshmallows, chocolate morsels, and butter or margarine in a medium saucepan. Cook over very low heat, stirring to be sure mixture does not scorch. Cook and stir until chocolate and marshmallows have melted and become a uniform mixture. Let cool slightly.

2. In a medium bowl, beat eggs, vanilla extract, and salt together. Sprinkle in baking powder; mix well. Stir in chocolate mixture. Add flour and all but 4 tablespoons of the nuts. Stir just to mix.

3. Spray or lightly grease a pan, and spread in batter. Sprinkle with remaining nuts.

4. Bake in the center of the oven 19–22 minutes or until a wooden toothpick

inserted ½ inch from the center comes out barely moist.

5. If desired, sprinkle additional mini-marshmallows over the surface of the brownie, and bake 1 minute more.

6. Cool completely in the pan on a rack. Chill several hours before cutting into 24 or 25 brownies.

CHOCOLATE SWIRL BROWNIES

A rich dark chocolate batter swirls through a lighter chocolate batter—a chocolate fantasy.

PREHEAT OVEN TO 350°F (340°F FOR GLASS)
9 × 13 METAL PAN

    2 *ounces unsweetened chocolate*
    2 *tablespoons unsalted butter*
  ½ *cup powdered sugar*
    3 *ounces Baker's German's Sweet*
       Chocolate
    1 *cup plus 6 tablespoons sifted*
       all-purpose flour
  ¾ *teaspoon baking powder*
  ¼ *teaspoon salt*
  ¾ *cup butter at room*
       temperature
  ¾ *cup granulated sugar*

  1¼ *teaspoons vanilla extract*
    4 *large eggs*

1. In a heavy small pan over very low heat or in a double boiler, melt unsweetened chocolate and unsalted butter together. Remove from heat, mix well, and let cool. Measure out powdered sugar, sift, and reserve.

2. Following directions in step 1, melt German's Sweet Chocolate; let cool slightly.

3. Combine flour, baking powder, and salt; mix well.

4. In a food processor or with an electric mixer, cream butter until fluffy. Gradually add granulated sugar, and beat until light and creamy. Add vanilla extract and then eggs one at a time, beating each in well. Stir in flour mixture.

5. Remove ⅓ cup batter to another bowl. Add to it the reserved powdered sugar and melted unsweetened chocolate mixture. Add melted German's Sweet Chocolate to larger amount of batter.

6. Spray or lightly grease a pan, and spread in about one-third of the melted German's Sweet batter. Drop remaining batters alternately, checkerboard fashion, onto first layer of batter; swirl gently with a table knife to marbleize.

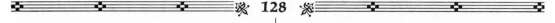
7. Bake in the center of the oven 22–27 minutes or until a wooden toothpick inserted ½ inch from the center comes out barely moist.

8. Cool completely in the pan on a rack before cutting into 16 or 20 brownies.

❖

CHOCOLATE CHIP OATMEAL BROWNIES

No flour in these brownies. They are both fudgy and crunchy and supereasy to make.

PREHEAT OVEN TO 350°F (340°F FOR GLASS)
8 × 8 METAL PAN

>   1 cup (6-ounce package)
>   semisweet chocolate morsels
>   ¼ cup butter or margarine
>   2 large eggs
>   ½ cup granulated sugar
>   1 teaspoon vanilla extract
>   ½ teaspoon salt
>   ½ teaspoon baking powder
>   1 cup old-fashioned or
>   quick-cooking rolled oats
>   ¾ cup chopped walnuts

1. In a small pan within a larger pan over simmering water or a double boiler, melt the chocolate morsels and the butter or margarine together. Stir to mix well, and let cool slightly.

2. Beat eggs and sugar together until light and foamy. Beat in vanilla extract, salt, and baking powder. Stir in chocolate mixture.

3. Stir in oats and nuts, and mix to coat each particle.

4. Spray or lightly grease a pan, and spread in batter. Bake in the center of the oven 25–30 minutes or until the top is crisp and puffy. Brownies will seem slightly liquidy but will firm up when cooled.

5. Cool to room temperature in the pan on a rack, then chill before cutting into 20 or 24 brownies.

❖

DOUBLE CHOCOLATE BROWNIES

A friend dug into her favorite recipe collection to give me this recipe. What more can be said about chocolate brownies with chocolate chips?

PREHEAT OVEN TO 350°F (340°F FOR GLASS)
8 × 8 METAL PAN

2 ounces unsweetened chocolate
¾ cup sifted all-purpose flour
1 cup granulated sugar
½ teaspoon baking powder
½ teaspoon salt
¼ cup butter at room temperature
¼ cup vegetable shortening at room
    temperature
2 large eggs
1 teaspoon vanilla extract
1 cup walnut or pecan pieces
¾ cup semisweet chocolate morsels

1. In a small pan within a larger pan over simmering water or a double boiler, melt chocolate; let cool to room temperature.

2. Combine flour, sugar, baking powder, and salt, and mix well.

3. In a food processor or with an electric mixer, beat butter and shortening, eggs, and vanilla extract together until smooth. Blend in chocolate. Stir in flour mixture just until blended. Fold in nuts and morsels.

4. Spray or lightly grease pan. Bake in the center of the oven 30–35 minutes or until the top is dry and a wooden toothpick inserted 2 inches from the center comes out clean.

5. Cool completely in the pan on a rack before cutting into 20 brownies.

SPICY FUDGE BROWNIES

These remind me of autumn and tailgate picnics. Maybe it's the cinnamon, nutmeg, ginger, and other spices often found in autumn baking.

PREHEAT OVEN TO 350°F (340°F FOR GLASS)
9 × 13 METAL PAN

4 ounces unsweetened chocolate
1 cup butter or margarine
4 large eggs
2 cups sugar
1¾ teaspoons ground cinnamon
½ teaspoon ground ginger
½ teaspoon ground cloves
½ teaspoon ground allspice
½ teaspoon salt
1½ teaspoons vanilla extract
1⅓ cups stirred all-purpose flour
1½ cups walnut or pecan pieces

1. In a heavy medium pan over very low heat or in a double boiler, melt chocolate and butter or margarine. Stir until completely mixed. Remove from heat, and let cool to room temperature.

2. Beat eggs, sugar, cinnamon, ginger, cloves, allspice, salt, and vanilla extract together. Beat in chocolate mixture, and mix in flour and nuts by hand.

3. Spray or lightly butter pan, and spread in batter.

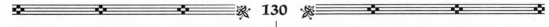
4. Bake 30–35 minutes in the center of the oven or until the top is dry and a wooden toothpick inserted 1½ inches from the center comes out barely moist.

5. Cool completely in the pan on a rack before cutting into 28 or 32 brownies.

SOUR CREAM-SPICE BROWNIES

A cakelike brownie with nuts and a spicy chocolate frosting.

PREHEAT OVEN TO 350°F (340°F FOR GLASS)
9 × 9 METAL PAN

  2 ounces unsweetened chocolate
  1 cup sifted all-purpose flour
  ¼ teaspoon salt
  ¼ teaspoon ground cloves
  ¼ teaspoon ground allspice
1¼ teaspoons ground cinnamon
  ½ teaspoon baking soda
  ⅔ cup butter or margarine
  1 cup packed light brown sugar
  1 large egg
  1 teaspoon vanilla extract

  ⅓ cup sour cream or yogurt
  1 cup walnut or pecan pieces
     Spicy Chocolate Buttercream
     Frosting (below)

1. In a small pan within a larger pan over simmering water or a double boiler, melt chocolate. Remove from heat, and let cool to room temperature.

2. Combine flour, salt, spices, and baking soda; mix thoroughly and reserve.

3. In a food processor or with an electric mixer, cream the butter or margarine until fluffy. Add the sugar in thirds, and cream until ivory colored.

4. Add the egg, and beat until smooth. Stir in vanilla extract, sour cream or yogurt, and melted chocolate; mix well. Fold in flour mixture and ⅔ cup nuts.

5. Spray or lightly grease pan, and pour in batter; smooth top.

6. Bake in the center of the oven 30–35 minutes, until the top is dry and a wooden toothpick inserted 1 inch from the center comes out barely moist.

7. Cool completely on a rack.

8. While brownie is cooling, make Spicy Chocolate Buttercream Frosting. When cool, frost and sprinkle with the remaining nuts. When frosting is set, cut into 24 brownies.

SPICY CHOCOLATE BUTTERCREAM FROSTING

- ½ cup semisweet chocolate morsels
- 1 tablespoon butter
- ⅔ cup powdered sugar
- ½ teaspoon ground cinnamon
- ⅛ teaspoon allspice
- ⅛ teaspoon nutmeg
- ¼ teaspoon vanilla extract
- 2 tablespoons light cream or milk

1. In a small pan within a larger pan over simmering water or a double boiler, melt chocolate and butter together.

2. Remove from heat, and stir in sugar, cinnamon, allspice, nutmeg, vanilla extract, and 4 teaspoons of the cream or milk. Beat until creamy.

3. Add more milk or cream if necessary to get a spreadable consistency.

❖

ROCKY-ROAD BROWNIES

The classic rocky-road combination—marshmallows on a chocolate base topped with chocolate topping.

PREHEAT OVEN TO 350°F (340°F FOR GLASS)
9 × 9 OR 11 × 7 METAL PAN

- 2 ounces unsweetened chocolate
- ⅓ cup butter or margarine
- ¾ cup sifted all-purpose flour
- ¼ teaspoon salt
- ½ teaspoon baking powder
- ¾ cup granulated sugar
- 2 large eggs lightly beaten
- 1 teaspoon vanilla extract
- ⅔ cup chopped walnuts or pecans
- 16 large marshmallows halved
  Chocolate Topping (below)

1. In a heavy medium pan over very low heat or a double boiler, melt chocolate and butter together. Blend well, and let cool slightly.

2. Combine flour, salt, and baking powder; mix well.

3. Stir sugar into the chocolate mixture, and then beat in eggs and vanilla extract. Mix in flour mixture and nuts.

4. Spray or lightly grease pan, and spread in batter. Bake in the center of the oven 25–30 minutes or until a wooden toothpick inserted 1 inch from the center comes out barely moist.

5. Remove brownies from the oven, and immediately top with marshmallow halves in evenly spaced rows. Return to the oven for 2 minutes. Remove from the oven, and set aside while preparing Chocolate Topping.

6. Pour topping over warm marsh-mallows. Cool completely in the pan on a rack before cutting into 30 or 32 brownies.

CHOCOLATE TOPPING

    2   ounces unsweetened chocolate
    ¼   cup butter or margarine
    2   cups powdered sugar
    ¼   cup milk
    1   teaspoon vanilla extract

1. In a heavy medium pan over very low heat or a double boiler, melt choco-late and butter or margarine together.

2. With an electric mixer on low speed or by hand, blend sugar, milk, and vanilla extract together. Stir in melted chocolate mixture, and beat until smooth.

HERSHEY'S
SYRUP BROWNIES

I adapted this recipe from one I found in an old pamphlet.

PREHEAT OVEN TO 350°F (340°F FOR GLASS)
9 × 9 METAL PAN

    ½   cup butter or margarine
    1   cup granulated sugar
    4   large eggs
    16 ounces (large can) Hershey's
        chocolate syrup
    1   teaspoon vanilla extract
    ½   teaspoon baking powder
    1   cup stirred all-purpose flour
    1   cup coarsely chopped nuts
        Chocolate Chip Frosting
        (optional, page 156)

1. In a medium saucepan over low heat, melt butter. Remove from heat, and stir in sugar.

2. Add eggs one at a time, beating each in well. Stir in syrup and vanilla extract. Sprinkle baking powder over the surface of the batter, and blend in. Mix in flour and ⅔ cup of the nuts.

3. Spray or lightly grease pan, and spread in batter. If you are not using frosting, sprinkle remaining ⅓ cup nuts over the surface of the batter.

4. Bake in the center of the oven about 25–30 minutes, until a wooden toothpick inserted 1 inch from the center comes out barely moist.

5. Cool completely in the pan on a rack. When cooled, spread with frosting and sprinkle with remaining nuts. When frosting is set, cut into 20 or 24 brownies.

ABBY MANDEL'S
TOFFEE FUDGE BROWNIES

These brownies are dark and moist with a surprising toffee crunch. Make them in a food processor.

PREHEAT OVEN TO 325°F

>   1 *cup (4 ounces) walnut pieces*
>   6 *chocolate-covered toffee bars*
>   *(6⅜ ounces total) broken into*
>   *small pieces*
>   5 *ounces unsweetened chocolate*
>   *broken into pieces*
> 1¼ *cups sugar (8¾ ounces)*
>   ½ *cup (4 ounces) unsalted butter at*
>   *room temperature and*
>   *quartered*
>   4 *large eggs*
>   ¼ *teaspoon salt*
>   1 *tablespoon pure vanilla extract*
>   ⅔ *cup (3½ ounces) unbleached*
>   *all-purpose flour*

Place the rack in the center of the oven. Grease a 9- or 10-inch square baking pan, and coat it with flour. Tap the pan to remove the excess flour.

METAL BLADE: Chop the walnuts and toffee bars coarsely by turning the machine on and off 6–8 times. Remove them from the work bowl, and set aside. Add the chocolate and sugar to the work bowl, and turn the machine on and off 6 times, and then process until the chocolate is as fine as the sugar. Add the butter, and process the mixture for 1 minute. Add the eggs, salt, and vanilla, and process the mixture for 40 seconds or until it is fluffy. Add the flour and the reserved nuts and toffee, and combine the batter by turning the machine on and off 4–5 times, just until the flour has disappeared. Do not overprocess.

Spoon the batter into the prepared baking pan, and spread it evenly with a spatula. Bake for 45 minutes or until a toothpick inserted in the center comes out with some moist crumbs clinging to it, but the toothpick itself should not be wet. The brownies may not have begun to pull away from the sides of the pan. This timing will produce fudgelike brownies. Bake for 3–5 minutes longer for firmer, cakelike brownies. Let the brownies cool in the pan on a rack, and cut them into 25 1¾-inch squares.

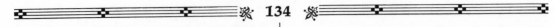
COCOA AND NUT BROWNIES

It's the corn syrup that makes this cocoa brownie stay moist and enhances the chocolaty flavor. Dutch processed cocoa is best for this recipe.

PREHEAT OVEN TO 350°F (340°F FOR GLASS)
9 × 9 METAL PAN

- ½ cup stirred all-purpose flour
- ½ cup unsweetened cocoa
- ⅛ teaspoon salt
- ¾ teaspoon ground cinnamon
- 1 cup broken walnuts or pecans
- ½ cup butter or margarine at room temperature
- 1 cup granulated sugar
- 2 large eggs
- 1½ tablespoons light corn syrup
- 1 teaspoon vanilla extract
  powdered sugar (optional)

1. Combine flour, cocoa, salt, cinnamon, and nuts; mix well.

2. In a food processor or with an electric mixer, cream butter or margarine and sugar together until light and fluffy. Add eggs one at a time, beating each in well. Beat in corn syrup and vanilla extract. Fold in dry ingredients just to mix.

3. Spray or lightly grease pan, and spread in batter.

4. Bake in the center of the oven 25–30 minutes or until a wooden toothpick inserted ½ inch from the center comes out barely moist.

5. Cool completely in the pan on a rack. Cut into 20 or 24 brownies. Sprinkle with powdered sugar just before serving, if desired.

·12·

BROWNIE LOVERS' DESSERTS

Strictly speaking, many of the desserts in this chapter are not brownies at all, but they are in the brownie family, so closely related that anyone who loves brownies would hesitate to pass them up. The Mississippi Mud Cake is dense, chocolaty, and redolent of good whisky—but still a cake rather than a brownie. Similar qualities characterize the soufflés, with their deep chocolate flavor and satiny texture. The Steamed Brownie Pudding, Baked Fudge, and two pudding cakes are just one step away from being brownies and will delight any brownie lover with all their chocolatiness.

Busy cooks will favor the crustless brownie pies that can be whipped up in minutes. They are basically a fudgy brownie baked in a pie pan and served in wedges, the perfect base for ice cream. They include the Fudge Brownie Pie, German Chocolate Brownie Pie, and Rum–Chocolate Chip Brownie Pie. These and other brownie desserts have evolved from the traditional square or bar shapes to unexpectedly delectable new forms.

For entertaining, you'll find some desserts so sumptuous that you may wish to serve only soup or salad for dinner. Then people can eat these desserts without scruples. For example, the Brownie Kahlúa Mousse Gateau—two brownie layers

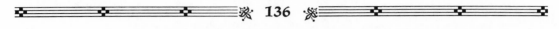
enclosing an excruciatingly rich Kahlúa mousse filling—is composed of ¾ pound of bittersweet chocolate, Kahlúa, cream, and eggs. In another incarnation, the fudgy brownie appears encased in a delicate cookielike almond pastry to become the Delicate Brownie Tart. The outrageously rich Fudge Brownie Pie in Mexican Chocolate Pastry sits in a pastry flavored with cocoa and cinnamon.

GERMAN CHOCOLATE BROWNIE PIE

The traditional German chocolate cake mixture of German's Sweet Chocolate, coconut, and nuts in a pie-shaped brownie.

PREHEAT OVEN TO 350°F (325°F FOR GLASS)
9- OR 10-INCH PIE PLATE

    4 *ounces Baker's German's Sweet Chocolate*
   ⅓ *cup butter*
   3 *large eggs*
   ¾ *cup plus 2 tablespoons granulated sugar*
   ¼ *teaspoon salt*
   1 *teaspoon vanilla extract*
   ½ *cup stirred all-purpose flour*

   ½ *cup flaked coconut (sweetened or unsweetened)*
   1 *cup chopped walnuts or pecans lightly sweetened whipped cream (optional)*

1. In a heavy small saucepan over very low heat or in a double boiler, melt chocolate and butter together. Blend well, and let cool to room temperature.

2. In a food processor or with an electric mixer, blend eggs, sugar, salt, and vanilla extract together. Blend in chocolate mixture. Stir in flour just to blend. Stir in coconut and nuts.

3. Spray or lightly grease pie plate, and spread in batter. Bake in the center of the oven 35–40 minutes or until a wooden

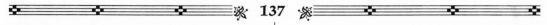
toothpick inserted 1 inch from the center comes out clean.

4. Cool to room temperature in the pan on a rack. Serve cooled or barely warm with whipped cream if you wish.

Makes 8 servings.

FUDGE BROWNIE PIE

This crustless "pie" takes just a few minutes to put together. It's best à la mode, and you can make it totally extravagant with the addition of chocolate, marshmallow, or raspberry sauce—and maybe even a cherry.

PREHEAT OVEN TO 350°F (340°F FOR GLASS)
9-INCH PIE PLATE

> 1 *ounce unsweetened chocolate*
> 3 *ounces semisweet chocolate*
> ½ *cup butter*
> 1 *cup granulated sugar*
> 2 *large eggs*
> ½ *cup stirred all-purpose flour*
> 1 *teaspoon vanilla extract*
> ¾ *cup chopped walnuts or pecans*

1. In a heavy medium pan over very low heat or a double boiler, melt chocolates and butter together; let cool slightly.

2. Stir sugar into chocolate mixture. Stir in eggs one at a time, beating each in well. Stir in flour and vanilla extract just to blend. Stir in nuts.

3. Lightly butter pie plate, and pour in batter. Bake in the center of the oven 28–33 minutes or until a wooden toothpick inserted 1½ inches from the center comes out barely moist.

4. Let cool to room temperature in the pan on a wire rack. Cut into 6–8 wedges to serve. Garnish with your favorite embellishments.

VARIATIONS

1. Stir in ½ teaspoon almond extract with vanilla extract, and use chopped almonds instead of walnuts or pecans.

2. Stir in 1½ teaspoons instant espresso coffee powder with flour.

3. Sprinkle top with a few additional nuts. A handful of semisweet chocolate mini-morsels may be added just after the pie is removed from the oven. They will melt slightly and stick to the pie.

RUM–CHOCOLATE CHIP BROWNIE PIE

Another fast crustless brownie pie. Very rich and great à la mode.

PREHEAT OVEN TO 350°F (340°F FOR GLASS)
10-INCH PIE PLATE

> 6 ounces semisweet chocolate
> ½ cup butter
> ¾ cup stirred all-purpose flour
> ¼ teaspoon salt
> ¼ teaspoon baking soda
> 2 large eggs
> ¾ cup granulated sugar
> 2 tablespoons light corn syrup
> 2 tablespoons amber rum
> 1 teaspoon vanilla extract
> ½ cup chopped walnuts
> ¾ cup semisweet chocolate morsels
> 2 tablespoons finely chopped walnuts

1. In a heavy medium pan over very low heat or in a double boiler, melt chocolate and butter together. Remove from heat, mix well, and let cool slightly.

2. Combine flour, salt, and baking soda; blend well.

3. In a food processor or with an electric mixer, beat eggs until thick and light in color. Gradually add sugar while beating 2 minutes or processing 70 seconds. Beat in corn syrup, rum, and vanilla extract. Stir in chocolate mixture. Stir in flour mixture just to blend. Mix in nuts and morsels, distributing evenly.

4. Spray or lightly grease pie plate, and pour in batter. Sprinkle with finely chopped nuts.

5. Bake in the center of the oven 35–40 minutes or until a wooden toothpick inserted 1½ inches from the center comes out barely moist. Cool on a rack at room temperature before cutting into 8–10 wedges.

FUDGE BROWNIE PIE IN MEXICAN CHOCOLATE PASTRY

PREHEAT OVEN TO 350°F (340°F FOR GLASS)
9-INCH PIE PLATE

> Mexican Chocolate Pastry (below)
> 2 ounces unsweetened chocolate
> ¼ cup unsalted butter
> ½ cup granulated sugar
> ½ cup packed golden brown sugar
> ¼ cup light corn syrup

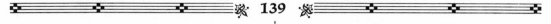
1   teaspoon vanilla extract
¼   teaspoon salt
3   large eggs
1   cup chopped pecans or walnuts
    lightly sweetened whipped cream
    or vanilla ice cream (optional)

1. Prepare Mexican Chocolate Pastry, and let cool.

2. In a heavy medium saucepan over very low heat or a double boiler, melt chocolate and butter together. Blend well, and remove from heat.

3. Stir in sugars, corn syrup, vanilla extract, and salt. Add eggs one at a time, beating each in well. Stir in nuts.

4. Pour mixture into prepared crust, and bake about 50 minutes or until filling is puffed and barely dry. The pie will sink when it cools.

5. Cool at least 4 hours or overnight. If you wish, serve with sweetened whipped cream or vanilla ice cream.

MEXICAN CHOCOLATE PASTRY

1   cup sifted all-purpose flour
2   tablespoons granulated sugar
¼   teaspoon salt
¾   ground cinnamon
1   tablespoon unsweetened cocoa

6   tablespoons chilled unsalted
    butter cut into pieces
1   egg yolk
1-2   tablespoons ice water

1. With a food processor or in a medium bowl with a fork or pastry blender, whisk together flour, sugar, salt, cinnamon and cocoa. Add butter pieces, and process or cut in butter until mixture resembles oatmeal. Do not overmix or let butter become warm.

2. Mix egg yolk with 1 tablespoon of ice water, and sprinkle evenly over flour mixture. Mix or process just until well distributed. Mixture will not yet form a ball. Turn out onto work surface, and press into a disk. If the dough is too crumbly, work in a little more water. Wrap disk of dough in a plastic bag and chill at least 1 hour.

3. Preheat oven to 425°F. On a floured surface or between two pieces of wax paper, roll pastry into a circle 3 inches larger than a 9-inch pie plate. Peel off one piece of paper. Place pie plate upside-down on dough, invert dough into plate, and peel away paper. Chill if pastry sticks to paper. If unpapered, drape pastry over rolling pin, and lift into the pan. Push pastry down into the pan, taking care not to stretch it. Trim pastry

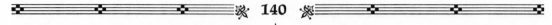
and flute edges. Prick entire surface with a fork, and bake in the center of the oven 12 minutes or just until pastry begins to color.

4. Cool on a rack.

DELICATE BROWNIE TART IN ALMOND PASTRY

A buttery nut crust with a light-textured brownie filling flavored with Cointreau.

PREHEAT OVEN TO 375°F
11-INCH TART PAN, PREFERABLY WITH
    REMOVABLE BOTTOM

    Almond Pastry Crust (below)
6 *ounces high-quality semisweet*
    chocolate
6 *tablespoons unsalted butter*
    cut into 6 pieces
3 *large eggs at room temperature*
⅔ *cup granulated sugar*
3 *tablespoons all-purpose flour*
⅓ *cup heavy cream*
2 *tablespoons Cointreau*
1 *cup whipping cream*
1 *tablespoon powdered sugar*

1. Prepare pastry crust, and let cool.

2. Prepare brownie filling. In a heavy small saucepan over very low heat or a double boiler, melt chocolate and butter, stirring occasionally. Remove from heat, mix well, and let cool slightly.

3. In the large bowl of an electric mixer, beat eggs until thick and light in color. Gradually add sugar while beating 6–8 minutes or until eggs reach the consistency of whipped cream. Sprinkle flour over the egg mixture, and blend in just until absorbed.

4. Gently blend in cooled chocolate, cream, and Cointreau just until incorporated.

5. Pour batter into prepared crust, and bake in the center of the oven 22–25 minutes, until a wooden toothpick inserted one-third of the way in from the outer edge of the tart comes out barely moist. The top will be cracked and slightly puffed. This is all right.

6. Cool tart completely in the pan on a rack, or cover with plastic wrap and chill until ready to serve. If the pan has a rim, remove it, and transfer the tart to a serving plate.

7. To serve tart, beat cream until soft peaks form. Gradually sprinkle in sugar and beat until stiff. Serve each piece with

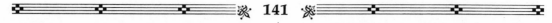
a spoonful of sweetened whipped cream, or pipe a circle of rosettes around the edge of tart and one in the middle using a no. 5 or no. 6 star tube on a pastry bag. Decorated tart may be refrigerated several hours.

ALMOND PASTRY CRUST

   ¾ *cup sliced almonds*
   1 *cup sifted all-purpose flour*
   2 *tablespoons granulated sugar*
   ⅛ *teaspoon salt*
   6 *tablespoons chilled butter*
   2 *tablespoons beaten egg mixed*
        with ¼ teaspoon almond
        extract
        remainder of beaten egg

1. Finely grind almonds in a blender or food processor. The grind should be fine but still have a little texture.

2. Combine ground almonds, flour, sugar, and salt in a bowl or in the work bowl of food processor; blend well.

3. Distribute butter evenly over flour mixture, and process with on-off motion or cut in with a pastry blender until mixture resembles oatmeal. Do not overwork or let butter become soft.

4. Sprinkle in egg mixture, and process 2 seconds, or mix with a fork just until incorporated. Mixture will not yet form a ball. Empty dough onto work surface, and press together into a disk, handling as little as possible. If the pastry is too crumbly to form a disk, sprinkle on as much as 1 tablespoon additional beaten egg. Wrap disk in a plastic bag, and chill about 40 minutes.

5. Roll out dough on a lightly floured surface to a circle about 14 inches in diameter. Ease dough into ungreased tart pan, and press dough down into the pan; avoid stretching the dough.

6. Trim dough ½ inch beyond the pan edge. Fold the dough edges over, and crimp ¼ inch beyond pan rim. Prick pastry at even intervals over sides and bottom of tart. Chill 10 minutes while preheating oven to 425°F.

7. Bake in the center of the oven 10–12 minutes, just until the pastry begins to turn golden. Cool on a rack.

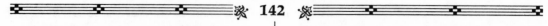
MISSISSIPPI MUD CAKE

A dense, chocolaty cake—not quite a brownie—redolent of good bourbon, with a hint of coffee. A fine Southern tradition.

PREHEAT OVEN TO 275°F
9-INCH TUBE OR 10-INCH BUNDT PAN

1½	cups brewed coffee or 2 teaspoons instant coffee dissolved in 1½ cups water
5	ounces unsweetened chocolate
1	cup butter
½	cup bourbon
2	cups granulated sugar
2	cups sifted all-purpose flour
1	teaspoon baking soda
¼	teaspoon salt
	unsweetened cocoa for pan
2	large eggs
1¼	teaspoons vanilla extract
	lightly sweetened whipped cream (optional)
	powdered sugar (optional)

1. Combine coffee or water and instant coffee, chocolate, and butter in a heavy medium pan. Cook over very low heat, stirring occasionally until chocolate and butter are melted. Add bourbon, and remove from heat. Stir in sugar, and let mixture cool 3 minutes.

2. Combine flour, baking soda, and salt; blend well.

3. Lightly butter cake pan, and sift or strain about 1½ teaspoons cocoa over the inside surface of pan.

4. Transfer chocolate mixture to the work bowl of a food processor or the bowl of an electric mixer. Add flour mixture, ½ cup at a time, blending well after each addition. Beat 1 minute with an electric mixer, or process 25 seconds. Beat in eggs one at a time; beat in vanilla extract.

5. Pour batter into prepared pan, and bake in the center of the oven 1 hour and 15 minutes for Bundt pan and slightly more for tube pan, until a wooden toothpick inserted into the center of the cake comes out clean.

6. Cool completely on a rack, at least 45 minutes. Gently separate cake sides from pan by wriggling cake with your fingers. Invert onto a large plate, shaking pan as you turn cake.

7. If you wish, serve with whipped cream, or pipe whipped cream rosettes on the top of the cake to decorate. Or sprinkle cake with powdered sugar just before serving.

Makes 12 servings.

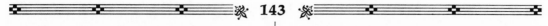
TUNNEL OF FUDGE CAKE

One of the chocolatiest Bundt cakes you'll ever eat. A fudgy center and a tender, moist exterior. If you overbake this cake, there won't be a tunnel, so watch carefully.

PREHEAT OVEN TO 400°F
10-INCH BUNDT PAN

    10   ounces semisweet chocolate
    1¼ cups butter, at room temperature
    ¾   cup granulated sugar
    3   tablespoons vegetable oil
            (corn, safflower, etc.)
    5   large eggs at room temperature
    1   teaspoon vanilla extract
    3   tablespoons light corn cyrup
    1¼ cups sifted all-purpose flour
    ⅓   cup unsweetened cocoa, strained
    ½   teaspoon salt
    1½ cups chopped walnuts
            powdered sugar (optional)

1. In a medium pan within a larger pan or in a double boiler, melt chocolate. Let cool almost to room temperature.

2. In the large bowl of an electric mixer, cream butter until fluffy. Gradually add sugar, continuing to cream until light and ivory colored. Beat in oil until smooth and creamy. Add eggs, one at a time, beat-ing each in well. Beat in vanilla extract. Blend in corn syrup, and beat mixture about 2 minutes more or until it is light and creamy. Blend in melted chocolate.

3. Combine flour, cocoa, and salt. Mix well, and fold in thirds into egg batter. Fold in nuts.

4. Grease Bundt pan well, and dust lightly with flour. Shake off excess.

5. Pour batter into pan, and bake in the center of the oven about 40 minutes or until a wooden toothpick inserted ¾ inch from the cake edge comes out clean and the top is dry.

6. Cool in the pan on a rack about 2 hours or until cake is just above room temperature. Loosen edges of cake gently with a butter knife or small spatula. Place a large plate over the cake pan, and in-vert cake, shaking to loosen.

7. Cool cake completely, and dust with powdered sugar if you like just before serving. Cake may be frozen wrapped well in aluminum foil.

Makes 14 servings.

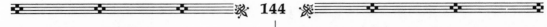
BROWNIE KAHLUA MOUSSE GATEAU

This dessert is for hard-core chocoholics. It begins with two modest layers of rather deep chocolaty brownies that enclose the richest imaginable filling of almost pure semisweet chocolate and Kahlúa, lightened just slightly with a little cream and egg. Select a really high-quality chocolate for the filling of this special dessert. The dessert freezes nicely. Cut while partially frozen or chilled; serve at room temperature.

PREHEAT OVEN TO 350°F (340°F FOR GLASS)
2 9-INCH ROUND CAKE PANS AND 1 8-INCH
SPRINGFORM PAN OR SOUFFLE DISH

> ½ cup unsalted butter
> 3 ounces unsweetened chocolate
> 1¼ cups granulated sugar
> 3 large eggs
> 1 cup sifted all-purpose flour
> 1½ teaspoons instant coffee powder
> ¼ teaspoon salt
> ¾ teaspoon baking powder
> 1½ teaspoons vanilla extract
>   Kahlúa Mousse Filling (below)
> 1 cup whipping cream
> 3 tablespoons powdered sugar

1. Cut circles of foil or parchment to fit the bottom of each baking pan, and line as directed on page 12.

2. In a heavy medium pan over very low heat or a double boiler, melt butter and chocolate together. Stir in sugar, and let cool slightly. Add eggs one at a time, beating each in well.

3. Mix flour, coffee powder, salt, and baking powder, and add to chocolate mixture. Stir in vanilla extract.

4. Pour into 9-inch cake pans, and arrange, evenly spaced, in the oven. Bake 18–22 minutes or until a wooden toothpick inserted 1 inch from the center comes out barely moist. Cool layers in the pans on racks to room temperature; chill.

5. While brownie is chilling, prepare Kahlúa Mousse Filling, and chill.

6. Invert chilled brownie layers onto plates, and gently peel away paper. Invert one brownie layer again, cut in half, and cut halves into 5 even wedges.

7. To assemble *gateau* in springform pan, place uncut brownie layer in it, trimming to fit if necessary. Cover with the chilled filling, and top with brownie wedges, reformed into a disk. Press top layer lightly and evenly to level filling, and remove any air pockets. Cover with plastic wrap, and chill.

8. To assemble *gateau* in a soufflé dish, coat bottom of dish with thin film of soft butter, and place the glossy side of cut brownie layer in it, touching the bottom of the dish. Cover with the chilled filling, and top with uncut layer, glossy side up. Press and chill as above.

9. To serve, run a knife around the edge of the springform pan or soufflé dish, remove pan rim or dip lower part of soufflé dish into a bowl of hot water a few seconds, and invert onto a plate; reinvert, and smooth out any excess filling around edges of *gateau*.

10. Whip cream, adding powdered sugar. Either pipe rosettes of cream onto each wedge, or cut each wedge, place on serving plate, and top with a rounded spoonful of whipped cream. Pass remaining whipped cream at the table.

KAHLUA MOUSSE FILLING

> 12 *ounces high-quality semisweet chocolate*
> ¼ *cup strong brewed coffee or ½ teaspoon instant coffee and ¼ cup hot water*
> ¼ *cup Kahlúa*
> 2 *large eggs separated and left to stand until room temperature*
> ⅓ *cup whipping cream*

1. In a heavy medium pan over very low heat or a double boiler, melt chocolate with coffee; stir until smooth. Remove from heat, and let cool slightly.

2. With an electric mixer beat egg yolks until thick and light in color. Slowly beat in melted chocolate. Stir in Kahlúa, and let cool to room temperature.

3. Beat egg whites until curved peaks will hold their shape when beaters are lifted. Whip cream until stiff.

4. Fold egg whites into cooled chocolate mixture, then fold in cream.

5. Chill mixture 20–30 minutes or until almost set but not firm before assembling *gateau*.

RICH BROWNIE SOUFFLE

Moist and cloudlike and not too sweet but very rich. The soufflé base may be made early in the day and set aside in a cool place. When ready to bake, warm over very low heat, and continue with the mixing and baking of the soufflé.

PREHEAT OVEN TO 450°F
1-QUART SOUFFLE DISH

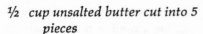
½ cup unsalted butter cut into 5
    pieces
4 ounces unsweetened chocolate
1⅓ cups granulated sugar
4 eggs separated and left to stand
    until room temperature plus
    1 egg white
1 tablespoon cognac, brandy, or
    orange liqueur
1¼ teaspoons vanilla extract
1½ teaspoons instant coffee powder
¼ cup stirred all-purpose flour
    vanilla ice cream

1. Lightly butter the soufflé dish, and
sprinkle evenly with sugar.

2. In a heavy medium saucepan over
very low heat or in a double boiler, melt
butter and chocolate together. Remove
from heat, and stir in ½ cup sugar. Blend
in egg yolks one at a time; remove from
heat.

3. Mix in the liqueur, vanilla extract,
and coffee powder; blend well. Stir in
flour until smooth. Set aside.

4. Beat the 5 egg whites until they are
opaque. Gradually add the remaining
sugar 1 tablespoon at a time, beating
only until curved peaks will hold their
shape when beaters are gently lifted. Do
not overbeat.

5. Fold one-fourth of the beaten whites
into the chocolate mixture. Fold one-half
of the remaining egg whites gently into
the chocolate mixture, and repeat with
remaining whites, being careful not to
deflate whites.

6. Turn mixture into prepared soufflé
dish, and sprinkle lightly with granulated
sugar. Bake for 5 minutes at 450°F, then
reduce oven temperature to 400°F and
bake 20–25 minutes or until soufflé is
puffed and dry on top. Inside will remain
moist.

7. Serve soufflé immediately with
vanilla ice cream.

Makes 6 servings.

BROWNIE-NUT SOUFFLE

I love to serve this with both coffee and
vanilla ice cream. Whipped cream is good,
too. Try using Dutch processed cocoa for
this recipe.

PREHEAT OVEN TO 350°F
1½-QUART SOUFFLE DISH

5 large eggs
6½ tablespoons butter
1 cup granulated sugar

5 tablespoons stirred all-purpose
 flour
½ cup plus 1 tablespoon
 unsweetened cocoa
1½ cups milk
1½ teaspoons vanilla extract
¼ teaspoon cream of tartar
¼ teaspoon salt
¾ cup chopped walnuts

1. Separate eggs, and allow whites to come to room temperature in the large bowl of an electric mixer.

2. Lightly butter the soufflé dish with 1 tablespoon of the butter, and sprinkle evenly with 2 tablespoons of the sugar.

3. Melt remaining butter in a medium saucepan; remove from heat.

4. In a small bowl combine flour and cocoa; blend well. Stir into butter, and gradually blend in milk.

5. Bring to the simmering point, and cook over low heat, stirring constantly until mixture is thick and smooth. Remove from heat, and stir 1 minute more; let cool about 10 minutes.

6. In the medium bowl of an electric mixer, beat egg yolks until thick and light in color. Gradually beat in 6 tablespoons of the sugar and vanilla extract until mixture is thick.

7. With clean beaters, beat egg whites until they are opaque. Sprinkle in cream of tartar and salt. Gradually add the remaining sugar, beating only until curved peaks will hold their shape when beaters are gently lifted. Do not overbeat.

8. Fold cocoa mixture into the egg yolks, and then fold in one-third of the beaten whites. Fold lightened cocoa mixture and nuts into remaining whites, being careful not to deflate them.

9. Gently turn into soufflé dish. Place dish in a larger pan containing about 1 inch hot water. Bake in the center of the oven about 1 hour and 15 minutes. Serve immediately.

Makes 6–8 servings.

ALMOND FUDGE BATTER PUDDING CAKE

A brownie pudding to eat with a spoon. This dessert makes its own sauce as it bakes.

PREHEAT OVEN TO 350°F (325°F FOR GLASS)
SHALLOW 1½-QUART BAKING DISH

⅔ cup butter, melted
1½ cups granulated sugar
1 teaspoon vanilla extract
¼ teaspoon almond extract
1 cup sifted all-purpose flour
½ cup unsweetened cocoa
1 teaspoon baking powder
½ teaspoon salt
2 tablespoons milk beaten with
    1 large egg
½ cup chopped almonds
1⅓ cups boiling water
    lightly sweetened whipped cream
    or powdered sugar

1. In a bowl combine 3 tablespoons melted butter, ¾ cup of the sugar, and the vanilla and almond extracts; blend well.

2. Mix flour, 3 tablespoons of the cocoa, baking powder, and salt. Add one-third of this mixture to the sugar mixture in the bowl, and stir in. Stir in one-half of the egg-milk mixture, another third of the flour mixture, the remaining egg mixture, and the last of the flour mixture. Stir in nuts.

3. In the baking dish combine the remaining granulated sugar and remaining cocoa; mix well. Mix boiling water and the remaining melted butter, and pour evenly over cocoa mixture in the pan without stirring.

4. Drop almond batter by tablespoonfuls over boiling mixture.

5. Bake in the center of the oven 45 minutes.

6. Cool about 25 minutes; the pudding will still be quite warm. Serve by spooning out portions and garnish with whipped cream or a sprinkling of sugar.

Makes 8 servings.

WARM BROWNIE PUDDING CAKE

Another spoon-style brownie dessert.

PREHEAT OVEN TO 350°F (325°F FOR GLASS)
9 × 9 METAL PAN

1 cup stirred all-purpose flour
⅔ cup granulated sugar
½ cup unsweetened cocoa
2 teaspoons baking powder
¼ cup milk beaten with 1 large egg
¾ cup melted butter
1 teaspoon vanilla extract
½ cup chopped nuts

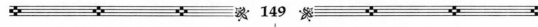
½ cup shredded or flaked coconut
    or ½ cup additional nuts
¾ cup packed golden brown sugar
1⅔ cups hot water
    lightly sweetened whipped cream
    or vanilla ice cream (optional)

1. Combine flour, granulated sugar, ¼ cup of the cocoa, and baking powder. Blend in milk and egg mixture, ¼ cup butter, and vanilla extract. Stir in ½ cup nuts.

2. Lightly grease pan, and pour in batter; spread evenly.

3. Combine brown sugar and ¼ cup cocoa; spread evenly over batter, and sprinkle with coconut or additional nuts.

4. Combine hot water with remaining melted butter and pour over batter, but do not stir. Bake in the center of the oven 45 minutes. Let cool 10 minutes.

5. Cut into 8–10 portions, and serve inverted onto individual plate. You may want to garnish the cake with a little whipped cream or soft vanilla ice cream.

BAKED FUDGE

I first fell in love with this at the Utica Square Tea Room in Tulsa, Oklahoma. I found the recipe in Tulsa's community cookbook.

PREHEAT OVEN TO 325°F
8 × 10 OR 8 × 12 METAL PAN

½ cup sifted all-purpose flour
½ cup unsweetened cocoa
¼ teaspoon salt
4 large eggs
2 cups granulated sugar
1 cup butter, melted
1¾ teaspoons vanilla extract
1 cup chopped pecans
    lightly sweetened whipped cream
    (optional)

1. Combine flour, cocoa, and salt; mix well.

2. In a food processor or with an electric mixer, beat eggs until thick and light in color. Gradually add sugar, beating 3 minutes more.

3. Blend flour mixture into eggs. Mix in melted butter, vanilla extract and nuts.

4. Spread batter evenly into ungreased baking pan. Set into larger pan, and add enough boiling water to come halfway up

the sides. Bake about 1 hours for the smaller pan and 45–50 minutes for the larger pan or until fudge is firm and a knife inserted in the center comes out moist but clean.

5. Serve warm, if you wish, garnished with lightly sweetened whipped cream.

Makes 10–12 servings.

STEAMED BROWNIE PUDDING

Steamed puddings are associated with Charles Dickens-style Christmas fare or early American cooking. This deep, rich chocolate delight, a cross between pudding and moist, dense cake, adds another wonderful dimension to the brownie repertoire.

To make the pudding, you'll need a large soup kettle with a cover, a rack or steaming tray to fit inside it, and a 2-quart mold with a lid (or use heavy foil).

   3 *ounces unsweetened chocolate*
  ⅓ *cup plus 1 tablespoon butter*

  1 *cup granulated sugar*
 ½ *teaspoon salt*
  2 *large eggs*
 ⅔ *cup milk*
  2 *teaspoons vanilla extract*
  1 *tablespoon baking powder*
  2 *cups sifted all-purpose flour*
 ¾ *cup chopped walnuts*
     lightly sweetened whipped cream
     or vanilla ice cream

1. Arrange rack or steaming tray in kettle. Place mold in the kettle, and pour in enough water to come one-third the way up the mold; remove mold, and butter inside well.

2. In a heavy small pan over very low heat or a double boiler, melt chocolate and butter together. Stir to blend well; let cool slightly.

3. In a food processor or with an electric mixer, beat sugar, salt, and eggs together. Beat in chocolate mixture until smooth. Beat in milk and vanilla extract. Sprinkle in baking powder; blend well. Stir in flour until mixture is smooth. Stir in nuts.

4. Spread batter into the mold; smooth top. Cover the mold with the lid or a double thickness of heavy foil secured with string. Place the mold on the rack

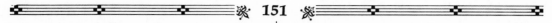
in the kettle, cover it, and cook in constantly simmering water 1½ hours.

5. Remove pudding from the kettle, uncover it, and cool on a rack 12 minutes. Place a plate over the top of pudding, and invert.

6. Serve warm, if you wish, garnished with whipped cream or soft vanilla ice cream.

Makes 8 servings.

Note: Pudding may be reheated by returning it to the mold, covering it, and steaming it again until warm throughout.

FROSTINGS

For frostings from other chapters see Index.

FRENCH CUSTARD BUTTERCREAM

  2 *egg yolks*
  2 *tablespoons heavy cream or*
      sour cream
 ¾ *cup powdered sugar*
 ½ *teaspoon vanilla extract*
 ⅓ *cup unsalted butter at room*
      temperature

  1. In a heavy medium saucepan, whisk together egg yolks, cream, and sugar.
  2. Over low heat cook about 10 minutes, stirring slowly and constantly until the mixture is light in color and thick and will cling to a spoon.
  3. Pour into a bowl to cool; stir occasionally. Or submerge pan containing custard halfway in a bowl of ice and water; stir until cooled.
  4. Beat vanilla extract and butter together until fluffy. Gradually beat in cooled cream mixture until light and fluffy. Chill buttercream about 15 minutes before using.
  5. Buttercream may be refrigerated 1 week or frozen 2 months. Bring to a cool room temperature before spreading.

Makes about ¾ cup or enough to amply cover one 9 × 9 pan of brownies or thinly cover one 9 × 13 pan.

QUICK VANILLA BUTTERCREAM

 1 *large egg yolk*
 5 *tablespoon unsalted butter at*
   room temperature
 ½ *teaspoon vanilla extract*
1¼ *cups powdered sugar*
 1 *tablespoon sour cream or yogurt*

1. Beat egg yolk, butter, and vanilla extract together until smooth.

2. Gradually beat in sugar until it is well incorporated and mixture is fluffy. Beat in sour cream or yogurt.

Makes about ¾ cup or enough for one 9 × 9 pan of brownies. Refrigerate 1 week, or freeze up to 5 months in a tightly covered container.

QUICK COCOA BUTTERCREAM FROSTING

 2 *cups powdered sugar*
 ¼ *cup plus 1 teaspoon unsweetened*
   cocoa
 ⅛ *teaspoon salt*

 ¼ *cup unsalted butter at room*
   temperature
 1 *large egg lightly beaten*
 ¾ *teaspoon vanilla extract*

1. In a medium bowl, combine sugar, cocoa, and salt; blend well.

2. With an electric mixer on low speed, beat in butter until evenly distributed. Gradually beat in egg and vanilla extract until frosting is smooth and creamy.

Makes enough to frost one 9 × 13 pan of brownies or two 8 × 8 or 9 × 9 pans. Will keep one week refrigerated or 5 months frozen. Bring to room temperature before spreading.

VARIATIONS

1. HALF RECIPE. Use 1 cup sugar, 2 tablespoons and ½ teaspoon cocoa, pinch salt, 2 tablespoons butter, 2 tablespoons lightly beaten egg, and ½ teaspoon vanilla extract.

2. MOCHA. In a full recipe reduce cocoa to 3½ tablespoons, and add 1 teaspoon instant coffee powder to sugar mixture.

PATISSIERE BUTTERCREAM

This is one of my favorite buttercreams. It is not too sweet, an unusual trait for homemade frostings. Try it with the Trilevel Decadence (page 104). The recipe cannot be made in very small quantities. But don't worry. This quantity is not unmanageable, and it freezes so beautifully that it can be kept on hand for the several recipes calling for it. Freezer life is two to three months.

>   3 large egg yolks
> ¼ cup light corn syrup
>   6 tablespoons granulated sugar
> ¼ teaspoon vanilla extract
>   1 cup (2 sticks) unsalted butter
>   at room temperature

1. In a medium bowl beat egg yolks until thick and light in color.

2. In a small heavy saucepan combine corn syrup and sugar. Bring to a boil, stirring continuously; sugar will dissolve.

3. Transfer syrup mixture to a heatproof glass measuring cup. Gradually add it to egg yolks while beating at high speed. When pouring syrup, aim for the eggs rather than the beaters or the side of the bowl. Continue beating until mixture cools to room temperature.

4. Beat in vanilla extract. Beat in butter a few tablespoons at a time until all is incorporated and the mixture is light and fluffy.

5. Chill about 15 minutes before using. Or refrigerate and bring to room temperature before using.

Makes about 2½ cups, enough for three 9 × 9 pans of brownies or two 9 × 13 pans.

SMALL-RECIPE FUDGE FROSTING

Just right for an 8 × 8 or 9 × 9 pan of brownies.

>   1 ounce unsweetened chocolate
>   2 tablespoons unsalted butter
>   1 large egg yolk
> ½ teaspoon vanilla extract
>   1 cup powdered sugar
>   1 tablespoon milk or light cream

1. In a heavy small saucepan over very low heat, melt chocolate and butter together. Remove from heat, and stir to mix.

2. In a small bowl, combine egg yolk,

vanilla extract, sugar, and milk or light cream; blend as well as possible. Stir in chocolate mixture until smooth. Let cool to room temperature. Test frosting for spreadability. If needed, add just a little more milk or cream.

DARK CHOCOLATE FROSTING

Extra chocolaty.

> 2 ounces unsweetened chocolate
> 3 tablespoons unsalted butter
> ½ teaspoon vanilla extract
> 1 large egg
> 1 cup powdered sugar

1. In a small pan within a larger pan over simmering water or a double boiler, melt chocolate. Remove from heat, and let cool slightly.
2. In the medium bowl of an electric mixer, beat butter, vanilla extract, and egg until well mixed. Mixture will not blend thoroughly.
3. Gradually add sugar about 2 table-

spoons at a time, beating until smooth after each addition. Beat in chocolate.
4. Chill frosting about 15 minutes before spreading.

Makes enough for one 9 × 9 pan of brownies. Recipe may easily be doubled for a 9 × 13 pan of brownies. Keeps 1 week refrigerated or 3 months frozen.

SOUR CREAM CHOCOLATE FROSTING

> ½ cup (3 ounces) semisweet
>   chocolate morsels
> ½ cup sour cream
> ⅛ teaspoon ground cinnamon

1. In a small pan within a larger pan over simmering water or a double boiler, melt chocolate morsels.
2. Remove from heat, and stir in sour cream and cinnamon until smooth and glossy.
3. Pour frosting over brownies while still warm, and smooth top.

Makes enough for one 8 × 8 or 9 × 9 pan of brownies.

CHOCOLATE CHIP FROSTING

   ½ *cup (3 ounces) semisweet*
      chocolate morsels
   1 *tablespoon unsalted butter*
  ⅔–¾ *cup powdered sugar*
   ¼ *teaspoon vanilla extract*
   2 *tablespoons light cream or milk*

1. Melt chocolate and butter together over very low heat.
2. Stir in ⅔ cup powdered sugar, vanilla, and cream or milk; beat until creamy.
3. If frosting is too runny, add up to 2½ tablespoons more powdered sugar.

❖

SEMISWEET CHOCOLATE ICING

A rich dark chocolate covering for brownies. It pours on like a glaze and sets to a fudgy consistency.

   5 *ounces deluxe-quality semisweet*
      chocolate broken into pieces
   ⅓ *cup powdered sugar*

  1½ *tablespoons unsalted butter*
   1 *large egg lightly beaten*

1. In a small pan within a larger pan over simmering water or a double boiler, melt chocolate. When melted, stir in powdered sugar until smooth.
2. Remove from heat, and stir in butter. Cool 3 minutes, and beat in egg until glossy.
3. Pour glaze evenly over brownies, and smooth with a knife or spatula.

Makes enough for one 9 × 9 pan of brownies or as a thinner glaze for a 9 × 13 pan.

PEANUT BUTTER FROSTING

An interesting way to vary a plain brownie like the Chameleon (page 26) or the Sour Cream–Brown Sugar (page 120). After frosting, dress up the brownie with a sprinkling of chocolate mini-chips or chopped unsalted roasted peanuts.

   1 *tablespoon unsalted butter at*
      room temperature
   ¼ *cup creamy peanut butter*

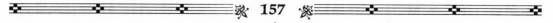
½   teaspoon vanilla extract
1¼   cups powdered sugar
1   tablespoon milk or light cream

1. Combine butter, peanut butter, and vanilla extract in a small bowl. Blend until creamy.

2. Gradually beat in sugar, and add enough milk or cream, about 1 tablespoon, to get a spreadable consistency.

Makes enough to frost one 9 × 13 pan of brownies or two 8 × 8 pans.

CHOCOLATE LEAVES

10   *large or 15 small fresh green
      leaves (camellia and rose leaves
      work well)*
4   *ounces semisweet chocolate*

1. Rinse leaves in cool water; pat both sides with a towel until completely dry.

2. Line a tray or baking sheet with waxed paper.

3. In a small pan in a larger pan over simmering water or in a double boiler, melt chocolate. Turn off heat, and leave pan in hot water.

4. Hold stem of leaf with one hand. Using a pastry brush or small spatula, spread a thin, even layer of melted chocolate on the underside of the leaf; do not let chocolate extend over the edges to the front of the leaf. Place coated leaves on the baking sheet chocolate side up; refrigerate about 5 minutes, until set. Keep chocolate warm over hot water. When chocolate on the leaves has hardened spread another thin layer of chocolate over the first; chill until hard. Repeat procedure until chocolate has built up to a thickness of about ⅛ inch. Chill at least 1 hour until very firm.

5. Twist several ice cubes in a towel. Cool hands by grasping towel-wrapped cubes. With chilled hands, peel away leaves from chocolate from stem end. Refrigerate chocolate leaves until ready to use.

INDEX

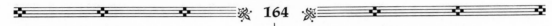